The Secret Place: Life Stories of Healing and Hope

I0531850

JUDY OWENS

ISBN 979-8-218-92100-2 (Paperback)

Judy Owens

Bookoflife1955@gmail.com

Preface

Putting my life on print is going against everything I was taught about family secrets. My family has always lived by the following mission statement: "what happens in our house stays in our house." The goal in keeping the family secrets were to not embarrassed or make the family feel ashamed by letting people know who we are behind the mask. As an imperfect person coming from an imperfect family, I lived what I was taught for years.

There were times I understood from the deceitful hands of friends why the family mission statement was significant in protecting our family values. Yes, imperfect family can have values. Some people love to weaponized your flaws to help themself feel superior and to bring shame with embarrassment to the family.

No longer am I allowing the calamity of my life to rule over me. No longer am I ashamed or embarrass. I break the power of darkness by letting it know I have the victory because of Jesus Christ. I am not who darkness say I am. Darkness is a liar. I am who God say I am. I am God's child wonderfully and uniquely created in his image. Through the name of his son and my savior Jesus Christ, I have the authority to resist and rebuke the devil. The blood of Jesus is on my door post. I am protected by the blood of Jesus; therefore, I will not walk in shame with embarrassment. I am free to tell my truth, and if my truth shows my family their true self beyond the mask, so be it; this includes self. I pray my story helps someone to be free from the bondage of secrets.

Christ told his disciples in Luke 9:23, "If anyone desires to come after me, let him deny himself, and take up his cross daily, and follow me." I understand that greater is He (Jesus) and that I need him to survive. Also, the bible declares in 1 Peter 5:8, "Be sober, be vigilant; because your adversary the devil walks about like a roaring lion, seeking whom he may devour." Verse 9 tells us to, "Resist him (the devil) steadfast in the faith."

As I document my life journey in chronological order, you will see pivotal moments when I had to pick up my cross and follow Christ in faith by resisting the devil to survive.

I was born at home on July 14th in Cook County, Chicago Illinois. The residential address 2848 west Adams is listed on my birth certificate as the name of the hospital. I was born during the baby boomers' era. In this era doctors made house calls. I was born the fifth child to a twenty-one-year-old single mother. As the doctor handed me to my mother, he tells her "It is a girl and she looks like a Judy." At that moment the name Judy was placed on my birth certificate.

Judy is a name of English origin and is derived from the name Judith, it is the feminine form of Judah. Judith has

Hebrew origins and means "He will be praised." I often wonder if God selected me before I was formed in my mother's womb to become the sacrificial offering for my family and for self. I know I was not created to atone for sin; Jesus cover that for us all. I often think about all the horrific things I and my immediate family have endured through-out our lives. My family used prescription drugs, illegal drugs, and alcohol to numb the pain of the horrific events. I chose a different route in numbing the pain. I found solace in talking to Jesus, praying, and praising God. At sixty-seven, as I reminisce, I realized I have always had a special insight in discerning beyond earthy vision. However, in my youth I was very naïve and unaware of this insight and God's presence in my life. I often thought God was displeased with me. I use to day dream about how to have a conversation with God. I wanted answers that I felt only God could provide. Looking back, I find it amazing how my young mind would think.

I can recall, at the age of five, living on the west side of Chicago on a street called Paulina. My siblings and I would attend the Catholic church on the corner of Addison and Paulina. I never recall my mother ever attending church with me and my siblings. She would give us that "you better behave yourself if you know what is good for you," speech before sending us out the door to church. Sometimes she would give us a nickel or a dime each to put in the offering plate at church. Many times, my siblings and I would stop at the small store to buy two for a penny candy to eat in church. We made sure to save at least three pennies to put in the offering plate. This routine of buying candy before church went on for a long time before we were ratted out by someone in the church. One Sunday after returning home from church our mother met us at the door with a belt in her hand. She did not ask us if we were guilty of eating candy in church, instead she administer the punishment for eating candy in church. I was more concern about who ratted us out than about the crime of stealing God's money for candy. Attending the Catholic church was my foundation to having knowledge of God. Although I did not understand anything Father O'Malley was talking about in church, the one thing I did gather is that God lives in the sky and Jesus is his son.

My best friend was a boy name Robert. Robert and I were in the same afternoon kindergarten class. The kindergarten classes were divided into two time slots. The morning classes started at 8:00a.m and ended at 11:00a.m. The afternoon classes started at 12 noon and ended at 3:00p.m. In those days, the early 1960s, it was common for young kids to walk the streets without a parent or an older sibling to accompany them. My older siblings walked the half of mile together to Brown Elementary School. Robert and I walked to school together in the afternoon. We both walked home after school at 3:00p.m with our siblings. Many times, I would play with my female friend who lived around the corner from where Robert and I lived. She was also in kindergarten; however, she attended the morning class.

One day I find a dime in an abandon car between the buildings where Robert and I lived. I could hear the ice cream truck ringing its bell on the other street parallel to my street. This meant that I had to walk the U-shaped block to caught the ice cream truck before it left the neighborhood. As I turned the corner to the street where my female friend lived, I could see a man sitting on the bench in front of her brown stone building. When I approached where he was sitting, he stopped me. "Hey, where are you going asked the man." I replied, "I am going to the ice cream truck on the next street around the corner." He told me to sit down next to him on the bench. At that moment, at the age of five, I knew this man wanted to hurt me, he wanted to molest me. Without any prior conversations or overhearing conversations, about rape, molestation, or not talking to strangers, I knew the intentions of this man. I tell this man that I needed to catch the ice cream truck before it leaves. He proceeds to tell me that he has ice cream in his apartment on the third floor and he would give it to me if I come with him to get it. I lied to him to get away from him. I told him that I would come back to get more ice cream from him after I go to the truck. He asked me, "do you promise." I replied with "yes." After buying my orange creamsicle ice cream bar, I went home the opposite way, cutting backway through the U-shape buildings. As I look back, I realized now that God wisdom and love was with me during a time when I did not think that God loved me. I am in awe of how did I know what I knew at that moment as a young child. I never told anyone about what the man said to me. I knew not to ever go to that building again or near it to play with my friend. I would often wonder if that man ever hurt my friend; however, I never asked her or told her what he said to me.

As I spent time with God going through chronological events of my life, God gave me his undivided attention which in turned help me to understand our omnipresent God. How he is everywhere at once. Therefore, I did not have to feel guilty that I was keeping him from anyone else who needed him. God spoke into my spirit; he let me know that we all have guardian angels assigned to us. These angels have authority given to them by God to help guide our footsteps by giving us divine wisdom on how to avoid the adversary who is always lurking to kill, steal, and destroy the hopes and dreams of God's children. These angels can only be successful when God's children's hearts are open to hearing. God told me, my heart was open to hearing him, this is why I knew what to do when the adversary tried to use that man to hurt me.

By the time I was seven years old, my mother had given birth to four more babies after my birth. One of the four died at the age of one. I was two years old when my sister died of crib death. She was sleep in the bed between me at age two and my older sister at age five when she died. For years, I had no knowledge of my sister who died in the bed with me. The remaining three of the four is two boys ages five and three and a sister one year old. A total of seven kids were living in our two-bedroom apartment on Paulina with our single mother. Us seven kids, living at home, ranged in ages from ten to one. My mother oldest son, my brother Jackie was being raised by his father

Shortly after turning seven, we moved from Paulina into a three-bedroom apartment that was walking distance from Paulina. Before moving from Paulina, I recall one of my mother's friends taking me to the Cook County hospital because I had a very bad bladder infection that caused me to break out with sores on my thighs. I do not recall my mother ever taking us kids to the doctor. It was always one of her friends or my older sister. The doctors at Cook County hospital put tudes in my pee-pee hole. They poked me with several needles. I was scared and alone. They gave me medicine and told me that I could not go home until I peed so that they could see what my pee looked like. My mother's friend was not in the room with me. I kept wondering if she had left me there in the hospital by myself and how would I get home. Finally, after hours of laying on the hospital bed, I peed. The pain and burning I felt from peeing caused me to scream and cry. No one was there to hold my hand or comfort me. It was a couple of days before I was able to sit without feeling pain. The move from Paulina went smoothly.

I have very little memory of this new apartment. Maybe it is because this apartment was haunted. Yes, it was haunted. My baby sister Denise, who was one when we moved in this haunted apartment was not walking yet. She did not walk until we moved out a year later. No one wanted to go into the living room except Denise and my mother. My mother bed and a couch was in the living room. The dining room was used as a family room. All the kids would sit in the dining room to watch TV or play games. The living room was always dark and cold. Denise would crawl into the living room. She would pull herself up to a standing position holding onto the couch as she cried for someone to put her on the couch. She would sit on that couch in the dark all day bumping her head back and forth against the couch. This was a daily routine causing the couch to have a permanent dent where she bumped her head. Things would move without anyone touching the item. Some items like my mother's house shoes would totally disappear. The apartment felt like someone invisible lived there and was always watching us. My mother always had a quick to anger tone in that apartment. One of my brothers cut me on my right shoulder with a hanger that he was trying to make into a sling shot. The cut was deep and bled a lot. I did not tell my mother about the cut because she never took us to the doctor anyway. We were used to getting cuts and bruises as kids. To me it was no big deal. My teacher looked at my arm briefly as she walked pass me. The next day she did the same. This time she tells me to have my mother give her a call at school. When I arrived home and told my mother what the teacher said, I received a whopping with an

extension cord. I could not understand why I received a
whopping. I did not do anything wrong. I was raised to not
question my mother; therefore, I could not ask her why she
whopped me. My mother never called the teacher and the
teacher never called my mother. I received a whopping with
an extension cord for no reason. Because I always feared my
mother and obeyed her, I was really confused about the
whopping. I did not understand how she could assume I was
guilty of doing something wrong when I was her only quiet
child that obey everything she commanded.

Because I was quiet and always obeyed, my siblings
would pick on me and called me names. They would say that
I was my mother's favorite. If this was true, I did not like
being the favorite. I was the one my mother asked to do
everything in the home because I did not talk back. I took
care of my younger siblings. I would feed them, prepared
their clothes for school, give them a bath, and comb my
younger sister hair. If my mother need something from the
store, she would ask me to go to store. Sometimes one of my
brothers would have to go to the store with me if the items
were heavy. My mother would have me scratch and oil her
scalp. Bring to her, items in the house because she did not
feel like getting up to get them. I had to peel the dry hard

skin from the heel of her feet when asked. Also, I would have to go with her to look for new apartments because she wanted to show the home owners that she has obedient kids. I could not understand why my siblings was jealous of me being my mom's favorite. I did not want the position.

My healing journey was embedded from each horrific event in my life. Surviving each horrific event with sound mind is the evidence of my healing; however, the breakthrough came at age sixty-seven. God was my rock during those aggravating years that I endured from my siblings picking on me and calling me names because they believed I was my mother's favorite child. God told me that he was near protecting my heart during this period in my life. What the adversary intends for evil, God used it for good.

I was elated when my mother found another apartment during the summer I turned eight. The new apartment was located at 16 S. Seeley Street, a few blocks from the haunted apartment. The calamity of living in this apartment will forever be engraved in my memory. My mother lied to the home owner, who did not live on the premises. She told the home owner that she only had three kids. The next day after we moved into the two-bedroom second floor apartment, the owner did a surprise pop up. The home owner walked into our apartment without knocking, she looked at my mother with anger in her eyes and in her voice. "Who is all these kids," shouted the home owner. My mother lied once again, replying "four of them is my sister kids. I am babysitter for her." My mother and the home owner went into the living room to talk. The home owner no longer looked angry when she left.

A few months after moving on Seeley, my mother had an appointment. She kept me home from school to babysit my younger sister Denise who was two years old. My older sister Carolyn who we all called Kale was eleven at this time and was allowed to go to school. A husband and wife lived in the downstairs apartment. The wife brother came from Mississippi to live with them. Soon following the wife brother was another man who came from Mississippi to live with them. I do not recall what this man relationship is to the couple. I think he was the nephew of the husband or of the wife. As I think back, he appears to be someone in his early twenties. He would sit on the pouch and talk to us younger kids. His name was Roy. He did not have a job or went to school.

As my mother leaves for her appointment, she calls for me to come lock the door. After locking the door, I turn on the TV searching for cartoons. My sister falls asleep on the floor. I picked her up and put her in the bed before going back to watching TV. Someone knocked on the door. I am not sure of the time lapse between my mother leaving and the knock on the door. My mother had me lock the door so I was not sure if she had her key. My mother never gave me the lecture of today's warning in not to talk to strangers or open the door for strangers. Initially I ignored the knock but wonder if it was my mother. I asked through the door "who is it?" The man downstairs whisper "Roy. Your mother told me to check on you when she left," states Roy. "And I have candy to give to you," Roy whisper. I pull a chair over to the door so that I could latch the chain on the door before opening. After opening the door with the chain latched. I asked Roy to show me the candy. He said that he needed to go to the store around the corner to get the kind of candy I wanted. My favorite candy was the two for a penny caramel square. Roy left to go get the candy. When he returned, I open the door with the chain fasten in place. I removed the chain after he showed me the candy. As I was eating the candy, Roy tells me to take off my clothes. I was wearing a dress and tights because I thought I was going to school that morning. I never changed my clothes after mom told me to stay home. "I do not want to take off my clothes," I whisper to Roy. "Why," replied Roy. "Because I am scared," I replied. "I will not hurt you," declared Roy. "Okay, but I am going in the closet to take them off," I replied. In the closet, I decided to only take off my dress, leaving my slip and tights on. I was scare to come out the closet. Roy kept telling me to hurry up when suddenly I hear my mother come in the door and yell at Roy. I heard Roy run down the stairs. My mother calls my name, "Judy!" "Yes mama," I replied. "Where are you," my mother shouted. "In the closet," I replied in a scared voice. By the time I come out the closet, my mother was standing near the closet with the extension cord in her hand. I was beat so bad with the extension cord, I had welts all over my body. I ran out the apartment down the stairs into the open-door apartment where Roy lived. The wife's brother who I believe is Roy's uncle was there watching my mother chase me and beat me with the extension cord. I could tell by the look on his face that he felt sorry for me. I desperately wanted this man to help me. He just watched, never saying a word, with a scare look in his eyes. I ran back up the stairs with my mother following close behind me, beating me. When will it stop, I thought to myself. Finally, my mother got tired and stopped. After she beat me, my mother asked did

Roy have sex with me. I told her no. I told her what happen and that I was scared to come out the closet. My mother never reported Roy to the police. Based on rumors, Roy family sent him back down south to Mississippi immediately after what happen. His family avoid running into my family. They end up moving a few months after the incident.

For years I hated the name Roy as well as any version of the name such as Leroy. I blamed myself for opening the door for Roy when my mom was not home. I felt like it was my fault. The shame of this incident stuck with me all my life until 2015 when I read Maya Angelou book titled "*I Know Why the Caged Bird Sings.*" Unlike me who was not rape, Maya Angelou was rape at the age of eight by her mother's boyfriend who lived with them. Maya Angelou kept what the man did to her a secret until her mother found the evidence in young Maya's underwear. Maya uncles handled the situation. The book does not state how Maya's family handled the situation; however, Maya stated that the man was missing. She left what could have happen to the man in the imagination of the readers. After reading this chapter in Maya's book, I begin to cry non-stop. I could not stop crying. In a way I felt relieved. Eventually I stop blaming myself and feeling ashamed. Suddenly, I realized that I was an eight-year-old girl who was expected to think and act like an adult. I realized that I was not protected as a child. My mother resolution in handling things that went against her expectations was to beat me. Although she never communicated her expectations to me, she expected me to know. I was a child, not a mind reader or an adult.

This incident was a tough one for me as I started my healing conversations with God. It was difficult for me to let go of the pain and shame because I felt it was my fault and I should had known better. God told me that there was a lot about my mother upbring that I do not know about. He said to me that "hurt people hurt other people because that is what they have been taught through experience. I say to God "but I have not hurt anyone, and I have been hurt." God told me that there is more than physical hurt and although I have not physically hurt anyone, I have hurt people. He further said that I would continue to hurt people if I choose not to heal. I asked God at that moment to help me to heal. I spent a year studying God's word non-stop, meditating on his word, listening to nothing but praised songs, praying without ceasing, and communicating with God by talking to him in my quiet time. God gave many confirmations regarding our conversations in many ways. I knew in my spirit that the confirmations were more than coincidences. During the healing process, I learn things about my mother's past that made me cry and have compassion and understanding.

My mother became pregnant with her tenth child when I was nine years old. I did not know my mother had a boyfriend. My new baby brother was born in 1968 five months before my tenth birthday. My twelve-year-old sister baby sat us for the three days my mother was in the hospital having her baby. To make it easy on my sister, no one went to school those three days. My sister prepared easy meals for us like hamburgers. We ate peanut butter and crackers every day for lunch, cereal for breakfast and a homemade hamburger for dinner. Us kids was so hungry we could not wait until our mother came home to tell her that our sister only allowed us to have one small bowl of cereal for breakfast, peanut butter on three to five saltine crackers for lunch and one hamburger without any sides for dinner. My mother asked my sister "why you did not feed my kids enough food?" My sister replied was, "I did not want to get into trouble because they would eat more than what was allowed."

I overheard my mother talking on the telephone to the father of my new baby brother. She asked him when was he coming to see his son. Also, I heard my mother asked him why he married her if he was not going to live with us. Later I heard my mother talked to one of her friends about changing her last name to her husband's last name, and that the only reason her husband did not want to live with us is because my mother did not drink alcohol and her new husband drink daily and was living with people who drink alcohol daily. It felt good to not be the only one in the family with a different last name. All my siblings were given my mother's maiden name. I was the only one with my father's last name before the birth of my new baby brother who was given his father's last name.

Being the quiet child, I was always to myself; not interacting with my siblings. I learned a lot about my mother's life from overhearing her talk to her friends in person or over the phone. I heard my mother tell one of her friends about an incident she had walking home alone one night from the bar. I did not know my mother went to bars. She was always home with us kids. Come to find out, while us kids where in bed sleep, my mother would occasionally go to the local bar. This is where she met her husband, Vernon;

my new baby brother father. My mother tells her friend that one night after leaving the bar, prior to meeting Vernon, a man grabs her by the arm and poked a knife in her side. This man walks my mom into the alley. My mother knew she had to react quickly. Her having height and weight on her side, standing at six feet, and weighting over two hundred pounds, she reacted swiftly by snatching the knife from the man hand and stabbed him several times. The man escapes her grip and ran. My mom told her friend that she had to throw away the white dress she was wearing because it was covered in blood. Although I was happy my mom was alive, I did not like hearing these types of stories. They made me feel sick to my stomach. Sometimes I would cry. I wanted to be strong like my mother without the experiences of having to hurt someone to protect myself.

During the winter of the third year living on Seeley, our kitchen caught on fire from the oven being used to heat the apartment. I was eleven years old when this happen. A friend of my mother who lived across the street on the opposite corner from where we lived had a small two-bedroom house. She had a large back yard. I do not remember this lady name therefore I will call her Mrs. X.

Mrs. X grew her own vegetables and she had chickens that she raised. Being displaced by the fire Mrs. X allowed us to live with her. Two days after the fire was out in our apartment, my mother, and my oldest brother slept inside the burnt apartment until we were placed in emergency housing. For the first time in our lives my family no longer live in a community that consist of brownstone homes and apartments. The Cook County Housing Authority gave my family emergency housing in the Henry Horner projects. My siblings and I had knowledge of these projects because they were directly behind Suder elementary school. My siblings and I attend Suder elementary while living on Seeley.

After moving into the Henry Horner first floor four-bedroom apartment my mother told us kids to not let the school know we had a change in address. The building we lived in was closer to Suder Elementary school than to the assigned school for our building. However, I was ready for a change. I had been in Mr. Gordon class at Suder from 3rd grade to fifth grade. I wanted a change in classmates and an escape from Brenda Crompton who was the class bully since third grade. I intentionally told a classmate in front of Mr. Gordon that we had moved into Henry Horner projects. Mr.

Gordon escorted me to the office after class to update my new address. The office staff informed me that they would have to put in transfers for my siblings and I to attend the school assigned to my building. Although the new school was a longer distance, at least I was away from Brenda Crompton. Although my mother was upset about me telling a classmate in ear shot of the teacher. I was grateful she did not whip my butt about it. Instead, she said my punishment for opening my mouth is the longer distant in walking to school. For once, I received a punishment I was highly in favor of receiving.

Living in Henry Horner was not an easy transition. My family and I had to swiftly grow in street wisdom to survive. We had to learn how to walk tough, talk tough, look tough, and whip people butt in setting a tone that declared in action, we are not the family you want to mess with. For the most part it worked. To gain respect living in the projects, one had to beat up, in a fight, the person who was sent to try your bravery as a person new to living in the hood. Because I was short and petite, I had to learn how to take down anyone larger than me if I needed to do so; therefore, I became a tomboy. I would play flag football with my brothers and I would wrestle them to the ground. I was good

at wrestling. I recall having only one incident while living in
Henry Horner projects where violence was used to protect
myself. This incident happened mid semester at McKinley
Middle School. I was in the seventh graded. McKinley Middle
School was only for students in the seventh and eighth
grade. One of my classmates was a boy who was kept back
twice. This meant that he was two years older than most of
the students, and he was also larger in height and size then
the students. In middle school, we still had to lineup like we
did in elementary school to go to lunch, the library, or to PE
class. The teacher would have the girls' line up first before
allowing the boys to line up behind the girls. The girls would
race to not be the last girl standing in front of the boys. This
is because the boys would touch the girl in front of them
inappropriately. The boys always allow the older guy in class
to be first behind the girl in line. In this incident, I was the
last girl lined up. This bully who should have been in ninth
grade took one of the girls knitting sticks from her desk to
use to hit me on my knuckles because I refused to turn my
back to him. When he touched me inappropriately, I lost it. I
blacked out. When I came to myself, my hair pick was in my
hand with blood on the tip. I had cut him on his arm. My
teacher took us both to the office. The office staff called the
ambulances and his parents. Back in this era, the ambulance

drivers were paramedics. My mother did not answer the phone when they called my home. The ambulances did not take the guy to the hospital; they cleaned his wound then put a large bandage on his arm. When this guy parents arrived, I heard the office staff ask them if they wanted the police to be called to press charges against me. The parents asked what happen. The staff told them what the students had reported to them. I was very scared. His parents took one look at me then said to the staff, this child is half the height of our son and is very small for her grade level; therefore, we know our son had to provoke what happen. No charges will be pressed against her. I was grateful and relieved that the police were not called.

Although we no longer attend the Catholic Church on a regular basis, my mother kept in touch with Father O'Malley and many of the Nuns, who would occasionally bring us food and clothes. I can recall wearing one of those black Nun coats with no collar during the seventh grade at McKinley Middle School. During the summer I turned twelve, my mother heard about a summer job program for kids fourteen and above. She took me, my older sister, and an older brother to apply for the summer job. My mother lied on my application by putting my age as fourteen. During that time, no birth certificate was required for the job, only a social security card was needed. My job was to be a teacher assistant for summer school first graders. My responsibility was to pass out and collect paperwork, pencils, have the class line up for potty break and escort them to and from the bathroom. Because the cafeteria was closed during the summer, I had to assist with passing out bag lunches. I was able to eat free lunch as well. I was paid $1.60 per hour. We were paid twice a month. We each received $60 per paycheck. My mother instructed us to give her $20 each per pay check and we were required to buy school clothes with the balance of our money. I was able to buy me a new coat before the winter of eighth grade. I worked summer jobs every year from the age of twelve. Every year the routine was the same, give my mom a third of my pay then buy school clothes with the balance.

My oldest brother joined a gang in one of our old neighborhoods when he was fifteen. I think he felt it was a way to show his loyalty to the neighborhood and guys where we grew up before moving to Henry Horner projects. My brother never stopped hanging out with his friends in the old neighborhood. His friends would often spend the night at our home in the Henry Horner projects. His friends were like family. My brother knew them for years. It did not become a problem until his friends joined the gang in their neighborhood. My brother joined because his friends had joined. Shortly after joining with his friends, the original gang members discovered that my brother lived in a different neighborhood and gang territory. They label him a spy and snitch. One night at one of the gang meetings, my brother was confronted by the original members. My brother pleaded his case then said that he would leave the gang and the neighborhood. He promises to never show face in their territory again. The original members ask the friends of my brother, "who else of you all want to leave the gang?" Only one of his friends raised their hand. Because the one that raised his hand still lived in the gang territory neighborhood, he was given a pass. However, a hit was put out on my brother. The hitman was my brother's friends who did not raise his hand to leave the gang. The friend had to prove his loyalty to the gang by shooting my brother. When the friend came, late in the night, to our apartment in Henry Horner projects, he was wearing all black. There were other gang members with him hidden from our sight. My sixteen-year-old sister answered the door. She was going to let the friend in when he said no; instead, he asked for my brother to come to the door. My sister called my brother to the door.

Before my brother could say a word, he was shot in the stomach. The rest of the gang members shouted out their territory name as they fire several rounds into the living room windows before running to the cars they came in. The only thing that saved my siblings and myself from the spray of bullets were the loose hanging silk curtains on our windows. The bullets bounced off the silk and hit the floor.

My sixteen-year-old sister ran to get my mother's shot gun. She did not know there was a bullet already in the chamber when she cocked the shotgun to fire at one of the guys. The gun jammed. My mother grabs a hand gun but it was too late, the gang members were gone. My sister call for an ambulance. My brother was rush to the hospital. My mother sent us kids to a neighbor house as she and my sister went with my brother to the hospital. I do not recall being scared. I was angry and I wanted to fight. I wanted to hurt the people who hurt my brother. I sat up all night at the neighbor's house. I could not sleep. I was infuriated with rage. All I could think about was *"how dare this person we called family shoot my brother."*

Housing Authority repaired our windows. I do not recall police coming to our apartment. I am sure they spoke with my mother and sister at the hospital. My brother was in the hospital for weeks. Once again, the Catholic Church came to our aid. They arranged for my brother to live with church members on the east side after he was released from the hospital. I remember going once to their home to visit my brother. These people were so loving, giving, and caring. They cleaned my brother wound and changed the bandage as needed. They sponge bath him and feed him in bed. I was in awe of these people who did not personally know us taking excellent care of my brother and hiding him from the gang members. My brother lived with them for nearly a year until me moved from the projects.

In my conversation to God, he reminded me of a previous conversation I had with him regarding how I did not understand how my mother could hurt me for no reason other than she was hurting. And when God told me that hurt people hurt other people. I say to God, the reason I did not understand was because "I have not hurt anyone, but I have been hurt." God told me that there is more than physical hurt and although I have not physically hurt anyone, I have hurt people. He further said that I would continue to hurt people if I choose not to heal. I asked God at that moment to help me to heal.

As God brought this conversation back to my memory, I realized there is different stages in how we hurt people or want to hurt people. We can hurt people emotionally, especially when they love us but we do not love them; yet, we use their love for our selfish advantage. We take advantage of them knowing that we could never give to them what we are receiving from them. I understand why God is showing me this stage because this was me in my marriages. God bringing this to me is helping me to differentiate the difference between the hurt I was feeling at that moment in time when my brother got shot. At that time, I did not feel fear; I felt rage because I wanted to physically hurt those who hurt my brother. I was hurting because my brother was hurt. Also, at that moment, I could see that my mother was carrying hurt from her past and that she was giving in her actions what she received. "God, I need you" is what I whisper in my thoughts. I am now seeking to lay aside every weight by picking up my cross and following you daily; because, I do not want the rage that I felt to consume me and define me as a person.

While still living in the Henry Horner projects, one of my younger brothers got into a fight. My brother beat up the boy. The boy's uncle was not pleased with the outcome of the fight. Therefore, he bought his nephew to our home demanding a rematch while he supervise. Because my oldest brother was recently shot, my mother was in protection mode. She got her gun and shot the man in his leg without any questions asked or conversation exchanged. The man went to get his friend and his gun. When they returned, my mother made all her kids get into the back room and lay on the floor. She engaged in a shootout with two men while my sister called the police. The men took off running when they heard the police car. Once again, we were sent to a friend's house to stay. My mother was arrested. She spent one night in jail. Father O'Malley asked his brother who was an attorney to help my mother. Because the two men was known in the legal system they were arrested and kept in jail.

Shortly after this incident, my mother realized my sixteen-year-old sister was gaining a lot of weight. My mother thought the weight gain was emotional stress because my sister was a witness to my brother being shot. My mother made my sister wear one of her girdles; but nothing helped. My mother decided to take my sister to the doctor. This was the first time I know of my mother taking one of my siblings to the doctor. I wonder was it because someone suggested to her, that she needs to be presence at the doctor with my sister. If that was the case, it was a good thing she was present. Because had my mother not found out from the doctor that my sister was nine months pregnant, it was a great possibility my nephew would have been born in a public bathroom.

A week after the pregnancy diagnose, my sister went into labor. Three days later when my sister came home from the hospital, I asked her where was her baby. My sister did not want to talk to anyone; she went into her room and closed the door. My sister went on a hunger strike; she refused to eat any food. She would buy bags of sunflower seeds, lock herself in her room and eat sunflower seeds all day. My mother had enough of the hunger strike. She whipped my sister using a belt, then she ordered my sister to go eat.

Once again, I hear my mother talking on the phone, telling her friend that she put my sister baby in the foster care system. My mother tells her friend that she refuses to take care of any kids that was not hers. One day my sister and I was alone, so I asked her about what my mother said. My sister confirmed that it was true, her baby was placed in the foster care system. I did not know what a foster care system was at that time. My sister tried to explain it the best she could. My sister says to me, "since my mother does not want to take care of my baby, I will no longer take care of her babies."

A few months after this conversation with my sister, we moved on the north side of Chicago during the summer of my fourteen birthday and my sister's seventeen birthday. My sister and I share the same birth month. Her birthday is eleven days before mines. One of my mother's friends' neighbors had purchased rental property on the north side. My mother's friend spoke to her neighbor about renting the second-floor apartment to us. They already had a tenant for the first-floor apartment. The owner of the property moved on the third floor of the brown stone. I was happy to be out the projects. My oldest brother was now allowed to come back home. He no longer had to be concern about running into the gang members that shot him.

I was enrolled in Roberto Clemente junior high school. I became friends with a girl name Rosemary who was also new to the neighbor. Rosemary and I had a couple of classes together. We walked to school together and became the best of friends. The summer of my fourteen birthday was the first year I did not have a summer job. At seventeen my sister was able to find work outside of the government ran summer program. To not give my mother money from her check, my sister bought me school clothes.

I was able to enroll in the government summer job program during the summer of me turning fifteen. I was assigned to assist at a child daycare center around the corner from where I lived. One day this guy came to pick up one of the kids, he asked me my name, then asked if he could talk to me outside. I told him no because I was working. He asked me what time I got off work. I told him at three; however, I ready did not think anything of it. I was surprised to see him standing on the steps of the center as I was leaving for the day. This man immediately starts asking me personal questions. He asked if I had a boyfriend. I told him that I was only fifteen and that my mom did not allow me to have a boyfriend. This man became a harmless stalker. He would walk me home every day. On weekends he would pass by my building to see if I was sitting outside. If I was sitting outside, he would sit there with me and anyone else who was sitting on the porch or steps, talking to us all like he was our best friend. I learned from the conversations this man had with us on the steps that he was twenty-nine years old and lived with a lady in her mid-thirties who had six kids. Someone sitting on the porch asked the man if he was the father of the kids. He replied "no." He proceed to say that he owes the lady gratitude because she gave him a place to stay. This man continued to stalk me by showing up everywhere I was at in the neighborhood. He never tried to harm me. On one occasion my mother was sitting on the porch and this man came to sit on the steps and talk to us all again.

One day I was at the laundry mat on the next street parallel to where I lived. When a classmate came into the laundry mat with an older woman. I immediately spoke to my classmate, "hey Lauren, what's up, are you also washing clothes?" Lauren looked at me and smile. She never spoke to me. She shakes her head in the position that represents no. The lady with her looked angry. The lady elbow Lauren like she was pushing her to move in my direction. Lauren did not respond to what the lady was trying to do. This frustrated the lady causing her to leave the laundry mat abruptly. The next time I saw Lauren, she explained to me that the lady was the best friend of the man who likes me, and that the lady told her that she wanted her to beat up this girl in the laundry mat who is messing around with her best friend's boyfriend. Lauren said when she saw it was me; she could not bring herself to do what this lady requested of her. I let

Lauren know that I was not messing around with no grown man and that I was not allowed to date.

One day my best friend Rosemary and I were riding bikes through-out the neighborhood when we both hear a gun shot near us. We looked in the direction of the sound. The lady that was trying to get Lauren to fight me was standing on a porch with three guys. She fired a gun in the air. When I looked in her direction, she pointed the gun at me, but the guys grab her and took the gun from her. The lady with the six kids hears about her friend shotting a gun in the air then pointing the gun at me. she sends her oldest child; a boy my age to invite me to a birthday party at her home for one of her kids. She told her son to let me know that she was not angry with me and did not want to bring any harm to me. I decided to go to the party with Rosemary. At the party I fellowship only with the kids my age. I did not say anything to the man who stalked me. I thank the lady for inviting me. After that party, I never had any problems with that lady's best friend. Also, the man who stalked me finally stop coming to my building to talk.

School was scheduled to open in three weeks. Our upstairs neighbors, the landlord, oldest son was preparing to return to college out-of-town. He was in the basement washing his clothes. Only the landlord had access to the basement. I was sitting on the porch alone when the landlord son asked me to help him in the basement. I declined, then he says to me, "so you are not a little bit curious how the basement looks?" I was curious to see what was locked in the basement. As I go down the stairs with him to the basement, he tried to kiss me. I rejected his kiss by pushing him away from me. He grabs me and tried to fondle me with his fingers. I told him that I will scream as I pushed my knee between his legs. He let me go, and I was able to run up the stairs to my apartment on the second floor. The next day he saw me coming home from work. He apologized to me and pleaded for me to not tell anyone. He said that him and his long-term girlfriend was going to get marry after they completed their last year of college, and if she was to hear about what happen she would not marry him. I told him if he never tried to take advantage of me again, I would keep his secret.

One week before school starts my mother allowed my sister's son, who is now two years old, to live with us. At this time my sister was eighteen. My sister finds a job working in an office as an assistant. Many times, she would not come home after work, she would stay the night somewhere else. She did not appear to care about her son being home with his family. She would behave like he was invisible.

I was always sensitive to energy as a child. I did not understand the magnitude of discerning people energy at a young age. As I grew older my sensitivity to energy was heighten. Shortly after my nephew comes to live with us, our family cat rans out the open back door. The cat did not return home that day. My younger siblings were upset. My mom tells them that the cat has natural instincts that would help him to find his way back home. A week after the cat was missing the cat spirit came to me in the middle of the night. Upon me feeling the cat presence, I woke from my sleep but I kept my eyes closed. I could hear the purring sound of the cat as it walked on the edge of the bed where I was sleeping. The cat spirit laid at my foot as it continued to purred. I remain still; I was afraid to move. Eventually I went back to sleep. The next morning, I told my mother that our cat was dead because his spirit came to visit me. One month after our cat died, I woke up to another spirit in my room. It was a tall slender African American man who was wearing blue jeans, a plaid flannel shirt with suspenders. I could not see his feet. It was like he was flowing about two feet above the floor. When I told my mother and described the man to her, she told me that it was her father. The day before I saw the man, my mother received a called informing her of her father's death. Later in life, I saw a picture of my grandfather whom I had never met in person, wearing the exact same outfit as his spirit when he came to visit me.

In the middle of the school year, my mother informed us kids that we were moving to the south side. I was getting tire of the constant moving. I was extremely sad to find out we were moving back into the projects. We moved into the Robert Taylor projects located at 4101 S. Federal Street, Apartment 510. The four-bedroom one bath apartment was a corner apartment across from the stairwell. My sister did not move with us, instead she moved in with her boyfriend. I became the surrogate parent to her son who she had no relationship with. After moving into the Robert Taylor, my nephew was enrolled in daycare. This is when I discovered my nephew's last name was the same as my mother's married name and my baby brother's last name. My mother said it was because my sister was under her insurance when she gave birth; therefore, the hospital automatically listed my mother's last name on the birth certificate.

As the surrogate parent, not by choice, I was responsible for feeding, bathing, and washing my nephew clothes. I would get him up in the morning, dress and feed him. Also, I would drop him off at daycare on my way to school and pick him up coming from school. I was enrolled in Wendell Phillip high school. It was difficult starting in the middle of the tenth grade. I did not make any close friends until the next school year. However, I became friends with a girl two years younger than myself who lived in apartment 506. Her name was Theresa Armstrong. We would occasionally talk outside on our floor or sometimes walk with each other to the store. My sister came once, maybe twice with her boyfriend to visit her son. The only thing she did was watched him play for a few minutes. My mother was getting a welfare check for my nephew. For this reason, my sister never brought anything for her son when she came to visit. My baby brother was two-years and three months older than our nephew. Those two was like brothers playing together. I do not recall my baby brother attending daycare at the same time of our nephew. I believe he remained home until he entered kindergarten.

My oldest brother was in the twelfth grade when we moved on the south side in the Robert Taylor project. He was scheduled to graduate from Dunbar Vocational High School that coming June. My brother informed my mother that he will be enrolling in the Army once he turns eighteen two weeks after graduating. I was sad to hear my brother would be leaving the family that summer to join the army; yet, I was happy to find a summer job on the west side after school end. Because Theresa was turning fourteen, she was able to get a summer job with me on the west side. It was good to have a friend travel on the bus with me every day. The government provided bus passes for Theresa and myself. The passes were good for a year. While I worked during the summer my mother was force to care for my nephew.

Once school started back in September of 1974, the old routine continued as usual. I returned to being a surrogate mother to my nephew. I was able to meet and become close friends with a few classmates. Two of my school friends lived in Robert Taylor. Debra lived in the next building. Wilma lived about a mile from Debra and I. Her sister would drop her off at school and pick her up or sometimes she would catch the bus home. Wilma was very athletic. She became a cheerleader and encourage me to follow my dream in becoming a pom-pom girl. I signed up to attend the after-school pom-pom girl meeting the next day. I was so excited. After signing up for the meeting I rush to pick up my nephew. When I arrived home, I asked my mother if I could join the girl's pom-pom team at school. I explained to my mom that I would have stay a couple of hours each day after school if I get accepted on the team, and that I would have to stay a couple of hours after school the next day to attend the meeting. My mother gave me her approval. However, when I arrived home the next day without my nephew my mother turn into the Tasmanian Devil. She begins to yell at me, "where is your nephew." I shouted back in a confused way, "I do not know, did you all not pick him up from child care." My mother beat me with an extension cord as she tells me to take my ass and go pickup my nephew. I am walking through the roles of projects crying as I go get my nephew. When I arrive, he was the only child left. The next day at school, my name was selected by the team captain as approved to join the team. Unfortunately, I had to declined, because there was no one to pick up my nephew for me.

My brother who was two- and one-half years younger than me had a problem with stealing. My mother would always defend him. She would hide what he stole and challenge the person who accused him. Eleven floors above us in apartment 1610 was the candy lady house. I never went to the candy lady house, but I was told she sells an assortment of different candy bars, individual bags of popcorn and potato chips and a variety of can sodas. My brother went upstairs to buy some candy. The candy lady purse was hanging on the door knob of the coat closet near the entrance door. As she turns to get chance from her chance box, my brother snatched her purse then runs down the stairwell to our apartment. The candy lady teenage sons came running down the stairwells after my brother. My mother protected my brother by hiding him in the back room. Instead of giving the candy lady sons back their mother's purse, she grabbed her shotgun and shot at them in the stairwell. The shot blows a hole in the wall of the stairwell. No one was injured. The candy lady called the police. My mother hid the purse by the time the police arrived. The police asked my mother if she has any guns, and did she shoot into the stairwells. My mother denied both questions. The police came into our apartment and looked only in the living room and kitchen. They asked my mom, who all lived in our apartment. My mother told the police herself and only the kids they see present lived in our apartment. The kids present were myself, my three younger brothers, which included The Thief, and my nephew. Before leaving our apartment, the police looked in the coat closet. The shotgun was in plain sight. I just knew my mother was going back to jail. I was in total shock when the police closed the closet door and acted like they did not see the shotgun. When the police left, my mother went to get the candy lady purse from hiding. No money was in the purse, only a lot of old papers. At that moment, I could not help but to think, *"we have become enemies with the candy lady and her sons over some old papers."*

At this point in my life, I begin to dislike my family. I thought about all the family fights, throughout the years. that my family had with other families in our neighborhood. I thought about the crime and stealing. I was tire of living this way. I wanted to know what it felt like to have a normal happy playful summer without the fights and crime. I recalled how I felt when us kids attended the Catholic church as a family. I might not had understood everything the priest was talking about but at least I felt safe. I decided to look up the address of the local Catholic church. The church was approximately ten miles away off State Street. I was elated that I had a bus pass from the government summer job program that was good for a year. I started attending the Catholic church every Sunday. I did not let the weather stop me from attending church. In church I would ask God to take away my sins and the sins of my family. Sometimes I would sit in church and cry. I cannot remember why I would cry. I think the tears were healing for me.

Around March of 1975 my sister moves back home. She had broken up with her boyfriend. By this time, my oldest brother had been listed in the Army for eight months. My sister moved into his bedroom. My mother moved my nephew toddler bed into the bedroom with my sister. My nephew was removed from my mother's welfare account to a separate account for him and my sister. After getting on welfare, my sister immediately applied for an apartment in the projects. She was approved for a two-bedroom on 43rd and Federal, only two blocks from where we lived. My sister moved in her new apartment in May of 1975. My nephew remained living with us. However, shortly after my sister moved, my mother informed the family that we will be moving to Los Angeles California before school starts back in September. My sister was asked at the end of July to come pickup her son. It was at that time she was informed by our mother that the family was moving to Los Angeles. My brothers assist my sister by carrying her son's clothes packed inside black thirty-gallon trash bags. My nephew was screaming to stay with me after hearing that he was going to live with his mother. He was holding onto my leg. One of my brothers had to pick my nephew up to carry him away. I was heartbroken. Occasionally I would call my sister to see how my nephew was doing. She informed me that it took him a month before he would talk to her. I was happy to hear he was adjusting to his new life.

We arrived in Los Angeles the beginning of August of 1975, two weeks after I turned seventeen. We had no preplan of where to live. My mother had the cab driver take us to a hotel downtown. The hotel was located on Hope Street near a large library. We stayed at the hotel on Hope Street for three weeks before moving to a cheaper hotel on skid row. School in Los Angeles started in August; therefore, my mother enrolled me and my brother, The Thief, in Belmont high school. The younger kids stayed with my mother during the day. Shortly after moving into the skid row hotel, my mother met a man at a store in the downtown area. She asked him if he knew of any low-income apartments for rent. She explains to him that we were new to Los Angeles and had no idea where to go look for housing. This man felt sorry for us after discovering that we were living on skid row in a run-down unsanitary, and unsafe hotel. The man promises to come pick us up on Saturday to look for housing after he talked to some friends who lived in the Jordan Down projects. I was extremely surprised when the man came to the hotel as promised. We all went in his car looking at apartments. The last place he took us was to his friend, Ms. Geraldine, who lived in Jordan Down projects. Ms. Geraldine was a single mother of three who moved to Los Angeles from Mississippi with her cousin, Ms. Carolyn. Ms. Carolyn also lived in Jordan Down projects. She was a single mother who had two kids. The cousins offer to help my mom get an apartment in Jordan Downs. The following Monday, my mother took a cab to the Jordan Down projects to apply for emergency housing. My mother was told, from housing authority, that it would take two to three weeks for us to be approved for the apartment. Ms. Geraldine allowed my family to move in with her as we waited to be approved for an apartment.

During our stay in the hotel, my mother had applied for her welfare to be transferred from Chicago to Los Angeles. I was truly grateful to Ms. Geraldine for allowing us to live with her for those two weeks. When we got our apartment in Jordan Downs, we had nothing but one luggage each of clothes. Ms. Carolyn sold miscellaneous items and clothes at swap meet. She talked to some of her swap meet friends and was able to get them to donate three old full-size beds with stained mattresses to us. Ms. Carolyn gave us some thick blankets to put on top of the stained mattresses and some fitted sheets to put on top of the thick blankets. My mom purchased from goodwill, additional bed sheets and covering, a kitchen table, pots and pans, and towels. We had to live without a TV for approximately two months. We sat in folding chairs to watch TV until my older brother sent my mother money to purchase a couch. At this time, my brother was station in St. Petersburg, Florida Army base. My mother purchased a used washing machine. We hung our clothes outside on the clothes lines to dry. By the end of September 1975, my brother and I were enrolled in David Starr Jordan High School. My other siblings were enrolled in local schools as well. I became close friends with JoAnn Brown, who lived near Mrs. Geraldine. Although JoAnn and I did not have any classes together, we both were in the twelfth grade. I would hang out at JoAnn's house every day. It was my escape from home. JoAnn had a large family. There were always some activities going on at her house, such as card games, domino games or just hanging out listening to music.

I was excited that we were settled in our apartment in time to celebrate Thanksgiving. I was looking forward to Thanksgiving because it was the one time a year my mother cooked food that we normally do not eat, especially baked sweets liked sweet potato pie, peach cobbler, and German chocolate cake. My mother routine was to the baked sweets and cook the Greens the day before Thanksgiving. She would prepare the turkey with cornbread dressing, ham and mac and cheese the day of Thanksgiving. On the eve of Thanksgiving, I decided to stay home rather than hang out with JoAnn. Ms. Carolyn tells my mom that the Catholic church on Compton Ave was giving out boxes of food for Thanksgiving. Following her normal routine, my mother sends me alone to the Catholic church for the food give away. The church was approximately one mile from our apartment. I could not believe my mother was sending me to ask for food on Thanksgiving eve while she was home cooking a feast. I felt like we were being deceitful to God asking for food that we did not need. Regardless of how I felt, I was always obedient to what my mother instructed me to do. When I arrived at the church, there was no one there getting food. I knocked on the side door of the church rather than the main huge entrance double doors. A priest opens the door then asked if he could help me. As I say to the priest, "I come for the Thanksgiving food giveaway," I begin to cry. At this moment guilt had overwhelmed me because my family did not need the food. The priest asked me, "are you a member of the church." I replied, "no." The priest informed me that the food giveaway ended a week ago and that they did not have any more food left in the giveaway. I am standing there looking at him crying feeling guilty. The priest asked me, "who sent you." I told him, "My mother sent me," The priest tells me to come in and call my mother so that he can explain to her that the food giveaway was over. I was surprised that my mother picked up the phone. I tell her that the priest wants to talk with her. I hand the phone to the priest. He explains to my mom about the food giveaway ending a week ago, then he proceeds to tell my mom that he was concern about me because I was crying. My mother asked to speak back to me. She cusses me out over the phone for embarrassing her and for crying. When I arrived back home, I was met with more cussing.

As I recall this period of my life. I think about how image plays a powerful role of delusional thinking and behavior, especially in my family. Us kids were taught to always show the image of our representative in front of people outside our home. We were raised with the "*you are not supposed to tell your family business mentality."* No family secrets were to ever be spoken or displayed publicly. We wanted people to see our glory only, without knowing our story. As a family, we walked around acting like we had it altogether. However, we all were self-sabotaging by wearing a mask to cover up, drug use, alcoholism, low self-esteem, depression, shame, and embarrassment. Although my mask did not include drugs and alcohol, the weight of the cover up was just as heavy.

I decided to attend on a weekly basis the same Catholic church I went to for the food give away. At this point of my life, I am still very naive with little knowledge on religion, Jesus and God. In my mind Jesus and God only exist at church; therefore, I had to go to church to visit them. The first Sunday that I attend church, I sat there crying through-out the entire service. I could not stop crying regardless of how much I tried to stop. Everyone kept turning around to look at me. I did not care about all the staring. In my mind I kept repeating, *"Jesus, I am so sorry I have not come to see you sooner. Please forgive me."* I felt comfort in going to church weekly. My attendance in church became less frequent after getting a job working at McDonalds around February 1976.

As a senior, school had become more financially demanding. My mother could not afford to cover any additional expenses outside of our household. My government class request each student to bring six dollars for a subscription to Time Magazine. The magazine was going to be used in class for discussion and assignments. My mother returned the note, from the teacher, with a note stating that she could not afford to pay six dollars for a magazine subscription. The teacher replied to my mother by instructing her to reimburse him twenty-five cents a week until the six dollars was paid in full. My mother being offended by the teacher comment replied by cussing him out on a note. Of course, I did not give that note to my teacher. This incident is what encourage me to get a part-time job. I put in an application at McDonalds. In the meantime, as I waited for McDonalds to call me for an interview, I went around the neighborhood asking parents if I could cornrow their daughter's hair for two dollar per head. One lady had three daughters and another lady had two daughters. I made ten dollars in one day. The teacher eyes bucked wide when I bought him six dollars in cash. I could sense in my gut that the teacher wanted to ask me how I got the money. He stares at me with this weird look for a few moments without saying a word. Fearful of what else was to come such as class pictures, year book, cap and grown, I became desperate to get a job at McDonalds.

Saturday morning, I washed my hair and while my hair was still wet, I rolled my hair with big blue rollers in preparation for Sunday church service. Once I was finish with my hair, I got an idea to call McDonalds and pretend that I was returning a call from them in regards to a job. The owner of McDonalds happens to be at the location. The guy who answers the phone says to me, "hold on, let me get the owner, it was probably him who called you." The owner answered the phone saying, "may I help you." I repeated to the owner what I had said to the guy who pick up the call. The owner giggled before saying, "this is the first someone calls to claim that they are returning a call about a job." The owner tells me, "You must really want to work." Then he says, "if you can come in within an hour, the job is yours." I tells the owner that I had just washed my hair and it was still wet with big blue rollers in my hair. The owner begins to laugh before challenging me to come as is with the rollers. The owner states, this will show how much you want the job. Within one hour I walked into McDonalds with big blue rollers in my hair. I could not believe that the owner put me to work immediately cooking French fries. I got the job. The next day I returned to work without rollers in my hair.

Working at McDonalds was fun to me. I got a chance to meet new people my age who did not live in the projects where I lived. I worked at McDonalds for approximately six months. Although most of my memory at McDonalds was suppressed, I do recall my friendship with a co-worker name Etta. I remember her to be a very bubbly kind hearted person who always appeared to be in good spirit. Etta did not live in the projects. She was the first female I knew, my age, that had her own car. I could remember on many occasions her giving me a ride or picking me up to attend some event that she invited me to. I valued her friendship and her bravery to come into the projects. I was grateful that she was that type of friend. Also, I recall my friendship with a co-worker name Leonard. He was a male version of Etta, with a kind heart and caring spirit. Leonard, the same age as myself had his own car. He too showed bravery coming into the projects to drop me off or pick me up for different events. Leonard and I formed an implied boyfriend, girlfriend platonic relationship. Being new to Los Angeles, California, many of my first experience to different venues and events happen because of my friendship with Leonard and Etta.

Some of my adventures with Leonard was Six Flags Magic Mountain Theme Park, Concerts at the Forum, movies at the Century Drive-In and occasionally eating out after the concert at Bob's Big Boy restaurant. Sometimes we would just hangout and he would take me to his parents' house. In my mind, Leonard was my first boyfriend; although, he never asked me to be his girlfriend. Years later, I learned that Leonard had given me the title as his girlfriend during the period we were hanging out together.

Working at McDonalds and hanging out with Etta and Leonard was the sanity that I needed to counter the insanity while living in my mother's home. My younger sister Denise and I would fight like cats and dogs. Although Denise was six years younger than me, she was a least five inches taller and ten to fifteen pounds heavier than me. Denise would take the new clothes I bought myself and wear them without my permission. Because my mother did not buy Denise new clothes, she would defend Denise and tell me to let her wear my clothes. Denise was an angry trouble child. Who was kick out of Los Angeles unified school district. She was bus to Compton unified school district, and eventually was kick out of Compton as well. Denise spends most of her childhood in juvenile centers and mental hospitals.

In July of 1976, after turning eighteen and graduating from David Starr Jordan high school, I spoke with an academic counselor at Southwest Community College. I wanted to become a nurse and needed to know what classes was required. I had to take a test to see if my academic skills qualified me for the required classes. I passed the test and was given a list of classes and the order in which I was to enroll in the classes. I selected three classes from the list that total twelve units for the first semester. School was to start the fourth Monday on August 23rd, 1976. I called my job at McDonalds during the last week of July and told the manager Mr. Bradley that I needed my scheduled changed because I will be starting college and needed the evening hours to study. Therefore, I requested Mr. Bradley to immediately put me down on the scheduled to work weekends day shift only. I explained to him that I came open in the mornings but I could not close because I did not have a ride home, plus I would need to be at school early on a Monday. Mr. Bradley informed me that he would change the schedule. That Friday before I was scheduled to open on Saturday July 31st at McDonalds, my other manager, who will remain nameless (Mr. X) because of his kids, called me to inform me that I was scheduled to work the closing shift and that I was placed on the schedule to open the following weekend. I told Mr. X that I did not have a ride home therefore I had to decline coming to work the closing shift. He told me that it was too late of a notice to get someone to cover for me. He assured me that he would take me home. I made sure he understood that my home was in the projects. He said that it was okay, and that he was not afraid to take me home in the projects. Unlike Mr. Bradley who was old enough to be our grandfather, Mr. X was approximately five to six years older than the teenage employees.

The closing staff at McDonalds normally consist of two female employees working the front counter as cashiers, and two male employees working the back as cooks and the evening manager. After locking the front doors, it would take the crew approximately two hours to clean and prepare for the morning crew to open. I do not recall the store hours. I believe we would leave around one in the morning. The two guy employees begin to heckle the manager when they see me getting in his car for a ride home. As the manager turns out the parking lot right, he was supposed to turn left at the light; instead, he turns right at the light. I told him that he made a wrong turn. He tells me that he must make a stop before taking me home. I asked him, "where do you have to go." He says, "I need to get something from my home." I say to him, "it does not make sense. You can get whatever you want from your home after you drop me off." He replied by saying, "I just brought the home that my brother and I grew up in with our parents and I really want you to see it." By this time, I am getting ready nervous and scared. I did not know the area well because my family and I had only been in Los Angeles, California for almost a year with limited transportation in learning the city. I was shaking in my voice when I told him that I did not want to see his house. He proceeded to take me to his home against my will. I sat in the car for a couple of minutes after he got out and open his door. I did not know what to do. Do I run to strangers in his neighborhood and trust that they would not be like him. I decided to take a chance with him because my coworker saw me get in his car. They would be a witness if something was to happen to me. What happen next caused me to suppress memory. At the age of sixty-five I started to have flashbacks of suppressed memory. I recall lying in a dark room on a mattress on the floor. I do not remember a bed. I do not remember the rape but I know I was rape when I became conscience. I remember thinking to myself, "why did he do this to me, I thought he was engaged to be marry to his fiancée; do she not give him sex." My rapist was lying next to me sleep. I am not sure of how long he slept before waking up to take me home. After remembering these thoughts and my state of mind after the rape helped me to understand, I did nothing wrong. On that Sunday after the rape, I call my job to say I quit without any explanation given. I never told anyone about the rape because of what happen to me at the age of eight when I was beaten by my mother with an extension cord for opening the door and letting the downstairs neighbor in our apartment while she was away from home.

Being rape changed me psychologically. I suffer in silence. I had blocked the rape from my eighteen-year-old mind. Although, at that time I did not recall the act of sex. My soil underwear confirmed to me that I had been rape. I feared how my mother would blame me once again, that eight-year-old girl in me went into protection mode in hopes of avoiding what happen to me ten years earlier when my mother beat me. Fear returns when I did not get my monthly menstruation cycle the second week in August it confirmed that my sickness was probably because I was pregnant. I was too sick to start school on Monday August the 23rd, four weeks after the rape. During this time, the city buses went on strike. It was a blessing in disguise because it kept my mother off my back regarding me not attending school. The morning sickness finally stopped three months after the rape. I hid my pregnancy from my mother. I had to find a way to get her insurance card so that I could go to the doctor to confirm I was pregnant. Because I had lost weight during the first three months of my pregnancy, I told my mom that I needed to go to the doctor to find out why I kept throwing up my food. The doctor confirm I was pregnant and gave me a May 9th due date. My doctor later changed my due date to the end of April. My son was born May 2nd, 1977.

My stomach was growing; I could no longer hide my pregnancy. I told my mother that I was pregnant. My mother talked about me so bad in front of my brothers, they begin to piggyback her in talking about their unwed sister. As my family question me about the father, I begin to believe the lie I told them. I told them that he was busy working two jobs to buy a house. Without saying, I implied that he was working to buy me and his child a house. My mother was not feeling that lie. She yells, "what that got to do with you. It is obvious you will not be living in his house."

Less than a month after my son was born, he got sick. He would scream whenever I touch his back. The ambulance was called to the house; it was early morning. I was in my pajamas and robe. After a brief exam they rush my son to the emergency room at St. Francis hospital. I rode with my son in the ambulance dressed in my pajamas. I only had my ID and insurance card. I learned that my son was diagnose with Spinal Meningitis. St. Francis rushed my son to Big General hospital. I was so scared I was shaking. No family member came to the hospital to support me. The nurses kept asking me was there anyone coming to support me. I told them no. The doctor told me that my baby would be in the hospital for a long time and that I should go home and come back the next day. I was at the hospital all day without food. I do not recall how I got home that evening. I think a neighbor came to pick me up. I took the public transportation bus every day to the hospital. The nurses would take time with me showing me support and encouragement. My baby had tubes in his nose and arm. I could not hold him. I would rub his hand and foot. He was fed through the tube in his nose that went into his stomach. My son was in the hospital for a few months before he was allowed to come home with me. He had to be taught how to suck a bottle again before they released him. I do not know who took me to the hospital to pick up my son. Before leaving the hospital, the doctors told me that my son would be developmental delayed and that he probably would not walk until he was around three years old or older. The nurses gave me information on the Regional Center and instructions on registering him so that I could get help with my son. Although my family was missing in action as I spent every day at the hospital with my son, God allowed the nurses to become my substitute family showing me support and love that I needed to get through in sound mind.

After coming home with my son, my mother told me that I needed to get my own apartment. By this time, I was getting welfare separate from my mother. I applied with Housing Authority for an apartment. I remember my friend Etta coming to my home after my son was home from the hospital. Etta was light in darkness, she enters our apartment with a bright smile saying, "I bought a few things for my God son." She had bought him a playpen, clothes, and some toys. I do not recall everything she had gifted to us. I was so grateful for her generosity. From time-to-time Etta would come get me out the house, by taking me with other friends of hers to a concert, and different events at one of her friends' houses. Of course, I had to pay my mom to babysit for me. It was worth me having some me time away from my family. When Etta asked me to be in her wedding, she made my dress for me. The dress was beautiful; I was proud to wear it.

After months of being on the waiting list, Housing Authority called me for a one-bedroom apartment located in Nickerson Garden projects. I did not want to move in Nickerson Garden away from my family; but of course, my mother took away the option for me to decline the apartment. The one-bedroom apartments were located on the end of the two-story row of apartments. I believe each two-story row of apartments had a one-story, one bedroom apartment on the end. My time living in Nickerson Garden projects was short lived before moving back home with my mother. I lived in Nickerson Garden approximately five months. During month three someone broke into my apartment while I was sleep. My son starts to cry for a bottle. I woke to go fix him a bottle. My back door, in the kitchen, was wide open. I believe my son crying scared the person away. I called my mother in the middle of the night because I was scared to go back to sleep. She came with my brother Big Al. They both moved my refrigerator against the window near the back door to prevent the intruder from prying the window open to unlock the door again. My mother left one of her hand guns with me.

All was good for another two months until a similar incident occurs. The intruder was on the cloth lines trying to pry open the window above the sink. Because it was no lights on in my apartment, the outside light caused the intruder silhouette to shine through the tan shade. I got my key and my gun. I eased out the front door making no sound, I locked the front door so that no one could enter as I creep around the side of my apartment to the back where the intruder was up on the cloth line. When I got to the back I shot at the intruder twice. I never seen anyone jump down and run as fast as the intruder ran. I unlocked my back door and went into my house. I never had any more problems with the intruder. However, after telling my mother what happen, she made me move back home. She said that she was scared I was going to kill someone.

After moving back home with my mother, I applied with Housing Authority for an apartment in Jordan Downs projects only. I was on the waiting list for a little over one year. During that year of waiting I felt like I was back in the Lion's Den living with my mother. My baby brother who we called "Bow" because he was severely bow-legged as a young child is ten years younger than me. He thought it was funny calling my son nigga because my mother would laugh each time he called my son nigga. Bow calling my son nigga irritated me; however, I did not have a voice in my mother's home. My son lost his identity for that year I lived with my mother. My mother joined my baby brother in calling my son nigga. Many times, in my thoughts I would yell, "shut the F up," yet nothing came out my mouth. I feared my mother, which caused me to not have a voice in speaking up for myself. My son did not crawl until he was almost two years of age. His crawling was slow in movement and short in duration. Although he made sounds, he could not talk or mimic word sounds. His hearing appeared to be okay. He would react to sounds and his name by looking in the direction of the person calling his name.

My son was two years old when I got the apartment in Jordan Downs. My son age is what qualified me for a two bed-room. My new apartment was two rows east of my mother's apartment in Jordan Downs. A larger apartment required additional furniture. In Nickerson Garden I only had a twin bed. I decided to put the twin bed in my son's bedroom although he was still sleeping in a crib. Because my mother used my kitchen table after moving back in her apartment, I had to purchase a new kitchen table. I went to the goodwill to purchase bed rails that could be used for full size mattress or pulled wider for queen size mattress. There was a small cheap furniture store on 90th and Compton

Avenue in Los Angeles where I was able to purchase a kitchen table and full-size mattress and box spring for the bed rails. The owner of the small store wrote up my order and scheduled it for delivery. With the owner was an older guy who was very friendly, and talkative with lots of questions. I thought he worked in the store. As the owner was scheduling my delivery he had to go in the back for something. The talkative guy asked me to write my phone number on the pad of paper. Although I had filled out the order form with my name, address, and phone number, I wrote it down because I thought he was the delivery person. When the owner came from the back, he gives me the date and approximate time my items will be delivered. The talkative guy walks me out the store to my car. He asked me my name. I thought that was odd because my name was on the paperwork. I told him my name. He told me his name then tells me that he lives around the corner on 90th. "Okay" I replied. Before driving off, I shout out the window, "it was good to meet you."

Two odd occurrences happen one month after receiving the delivery of my kitchen table and mattresses. The first odd occurrence is when my mother tells me, in two months she will be going to Chicago to bring my sister and nephew back to California to live, and that my sister will be living with me, and my nephew will be living with her. At this point, although I was twenty years old, I was still under the influence of my mother commands. I was happy my mother gave me two months to prepare for the arrival of my sister. By the second month I had saved two hundred dollars. The good thing about living in the hood, one could always find a street vendor selling anything a person could imagine. On a 103rd street, a vendor had an empty lot rope off as he sold matching love seats and couch. I was able to purchase a royal blue crushed velvet matching love seat and couch for one hundred and seventy-five dollars. The street vendor had an empty truck and two drivers for immediate delivery. The drivers follow me the one-mile home. Cash was paid upon delivery. My living room was complete with couch, love seat, and TV on a wood stand. Although I did not have any end tables or coffee table, I was happy my living room was not empty.

The second odd occurrence was the phone call I received from the talkative guy who was at the furniture store on 90th and Compton Avenue. A second after saying "hello" this guy begins to talk to me like he knew me for years. He starts the conversation with, "hey Judy, long time no hear. How have things been going? I missed you. I have been thinking about you since our last encounter; therefore, I decided to give you a call." I was thinking "who the heck is this," but what came out my mouth was, "who is this?" He says his name. I will call him Mr. H. Before allowing me to ask him any questions, Mr. H begins to tell me his whole life story of becoming a single father and owning his home. Finally, he took a breath and I was able to ask him his age. He told me that he was thirty-five. Although he was a good-looking man, he was too old for me. I say to him, "Mr. H you are fifteen years older than me." He tells me that he like younger women because he was young at heart and older women was too fussy for him. He asked me if I had a boyfriend. I replied no and I am not looking for one. Then he asked if he could call me from time to time to check on me as a friend. Before I could reply, he tells me that anytime I need help with anything, my car, moving furniture, a ride, something repaired, to give him a call and he will take care of it as a friend. I thought for a few seconds about how good it would be to have a handy man in case I needed help. I ended the call with, "sure you can call me from time to time to check on me as a friend." Mr. H. called me every two to three months just to talk and check on me.

Two weeks after my sister arrived in California, she applied for housing with Housing Authority. She lived with me a little over a year before getting a two-bedroom apartment in Imperial Courts projects, which was a ten-minute drive from Jordan Downs. A couple of months before my sister moved into her apartment, Leonard came to my apartment in Jordan Downs. By this time, Leonard and I both were twenty-one years old. I do not recall how he knew where I lived or how he got my new phone number. Or if we talked after the rape incident. I could not recall talking to him about what happen to me or having a conversation with him about our relationship ending. I feared asking him any questions because I did not want him to see me differently than who he had known me to be. I remember it feeling like old times when he came to visit. Also, I remember asking my sister if she could babysit my son. Leonard and I went on a date; however, I cannot recall where we went. Through-out the years, I would run into Leonard from time to time. He was forever in my heart.

Once my son turns three years old, the Regional Center arranged for him to attend a school that specialized in developmentally delayed children. My son was in school for three hours each weekday, Monday through Friday, excluding holidays. The bus ride extends my son time away from home by thirty minutes each way. This allowed me four hours per day to run errands or go to the doctor. The school helped my son in learning how to pull himself up to a standing position and to make slow sturdy steps by holding on to the wall or using a walker. My son mainly crawled on his own without help. A wheel chair was used for public mobility. My son could not operate his wheelchair. Someone had to push him.

Many times, I would sit in my apartment day dreaming about working in a big office. I wanted to know what it was like to have an office job. Sometimes, I often would wonder, had I not been rape, would I now be working as a nurse. These thoughts would make me sad. Although I loved my son, I felt like I was robbed of my life because of my rapist. I felt like my son and I were punished for something we did not do. Many times, I would think was my son and I punished for my sins and the sins of my family. I would say to God, why was I chosen for this punishment. My family appeared to freely live their life, while I was limited to what I could do. I would read the bible often. I would ask God; how do I do what this bible is saying. Can I really move a mountain with faith. Is it true, that if I believe in my heart that I already have what I am asking God for before I receive it then I will receive it. I would asked God these questions as I read the bible. I did not like sitting around feeling sorry for myself. I begin to look forward to Mr. H phone calls just to have someone to talk to. He became my friend. He offered to help me with my son anytime I needed him. I allowed Mr. H to come visit me at my apartment. Sometimes I would go visit Mr. H at his house when my son was at school. He became the only consistent friend I had. By the time my son was four years old, and I was twenty-two, Mr. H expressed his love for me. We were not intimate friends when Mr. H expressed his love for me. I almost fell out my seat when he asked me to move in with him immediately after expressing his love for me. Although, I did not feel the same way about Mr. H as he felt for me, I said yes to moving in with him. I knew this meant that I was agreeing to being his girlfriend. I enjoyed living with Mr. H. I especially enjoyed having someone to help me and someone to have adult conversation with. Mr. H wanted us to have a child together. I could see that he was a good father to the three kids he was raising alone; therefore, I agreed to get pregnant. We got engaged to be marry after the birth of our baby. Almost a year after moving into Mr. H house, I gave birth to my second son, Junior, and I married Mr. H.

Things were going well during my pregnancy. It was after I said "I do" and became the Mrs., the relationship changed. Mr. H was a stay-at-home dad. He received government assistance in raising his kids. Mr. H spent his life living inside his garage also known as his man cave. In the man cave Mr. H would play cards and dominoes with the young guys from the neighborhood. He would also flirt with the young girls. One day I was sitting in my mommy rocking chair with the baby. My chair was near the window so that I could look out and sight see as I rock the baby to sleep or just enjoying bonding time with the baby while my oldest son was at school. Sometimes I would rock my oldest son in the chair so that he did not feel left out. Anyhow, one day as I am rocking the baby to sleep, I see the girl next door drive my car into the driveway. Mr. H and I both had keys to our cars. The girl next door is eighteen and lives with her single mother. She does not work or go to school. She is always outside sitting on her front porch. Most people use her nickname Candy when addressing her. I waited until I saw Candy leave before I went to confront Mr. H for allowing her to drive my car without asking my permission. Mr. H felt that he did not need my permission since Candy was running an errand for him. I asked him, why she did not drive your car. His reply was "because it is a truck."

Mr. H daughters and I was close in age. I am five years older than his oldest daughter. Mr. H did not like when his daughters would tell me about his affairs. One of his daughters caught Mr. H having sex with Candy in the garage. I knew he was having sex with young girls in the garage; but I did not care. I did not love Mr. H in a romantic way. I liked him as a person. Mr. H was very consistent in getting my son off his school bus every day. He would flirt and talk to the young female bus driver for about ten minutes each day as she dropped off my son. This young bus driver did not care about the kids left on a hot bus while she playfully giggles with my husband every day.

During my marriage, my older sister was the only relative I would talk too. This is because my family once again criticized me harshly for moving in with Mr. H and for getting pregnant with my second child. My baby brother Bow had the nerve to call me on the phone and yell at me like he was my daddy regarding me marrying my husband without his permission and for getting pregnant with a second child. Yes, you heard me correctly, Bow had the nerve to reprimand me verbally about not getting his permission to get marry and have another child. This is why I only communicated with my older sister.

I was assigned a social worker through the Regional Center. The social worker would visit twice a year checking to see if my son's needs were being met also checking in making sure my emotional and mental health was stable as I raised a special need child. Every time the worker would come out for a home visit, she would never fail to talk to me about placement for my son so that I could take advantage of opportunities like going to school or becoming employed. I always replied with the same answer. I would tell her that it sounds good; however, I would feel like a bad mom who abandon her son. The worker asked me; do I still daydream about working in an office. I told her yes, but not as much now that I have a husband and another son to raise.

My routine with Mr. H became boring. I was tired of watching him flirt with young girls and have sex in the garage with them. I never socialize with anyone other than my older sister. The routine was starting to psychologically affect me. The social worker came for her routine visit shortly after my son seventh birthday in May 1984. This time when she discussed placement with me, I begin to pay more attention to what she was saying. I asked a lot of questions about the program. She offers to set up for me to visit with my son a placement location not far from me. I agreed. When I arrive with my son to the placement location, there was another mother who had twin special need kids. One girl and one boy. Both her kids were wheelchair bonded like my son. I could not image having two with no help. The owner of the placement center had three locations which were large houses owned by him. The owner explained that it was a family business past down from his grandparents to his parents and now to him. I was able to visit two of his locations. Each location was clean. The recipients had their own bed, dresser, and closet space. They could freely move about. They had a play room and a TV room and outside workers who were trained in caring for special need people. I begin to feel better about placement. I asked the worker to give me a little time to make sure it is what I want to do. I thought about placement every day for a month. The worker assured me that I could always have my son return home should I change my mind. I decided to give placement a try. Mr. H went with me to take my son to placement. We both cried when we left my son. We both would often go visit. Although placement was going well with my son I would feel psychologically drained each time, I left from visiting him. I would get weak and had to lay in bed for about two days before my strength would come back. My family was my worst critics when I told them that my son was in placement.

They called me a bad mother who threw away my son. They had a lot to say for people who did not help me with my son. For years, even after we were divorce, Mr. H would occasionally go visit my son and would always give me a good report as to how my son was doing. God revealed my growth in reading his word as my family criticized me and label me a bad mom. Their words had no power over me anymore. Their words no longer pierced my heart with pain. I learned to hate the darkness that used them as I continued to love them as my family.

A few weeks after placing my son, I enrolled Junior in daycare and myself into a six-month career college program. I learned how to type and ten-key by touch. After completing career college in November of 1984, I got a job in December of 1984 working at Mitsubishi Electronics. I started as a temp employee working as a data entry clerk in the Order Control Department. I was hire permanently as a full-time employee three months after working as a temp employee. I was so proud of myself for catching on quickly in learning my job assignment and for learning how to navigate the company's computer system. When I started in 1984, I became the third wheel in the Order Control department. There were two coordinators, and myself as the data entry clerk. Us three employees reported to the Order Control manager who had a secretary.

Things were going well a home when I first started working. I got off work every day at four-thirty. I would come straight home to immediately start cooking dinner after picking up Junior from daycare. Although Mr. H was still getting government assistance and still spending his days in the garage, he refused to pick up Junior from daycare. The daycare was located inside the church around the corner from where we lived. Junior had to be picked up by six p.m. There were times I wanted to stop by the store after getting off work; however, I could not stop at the store because I had to go directly to daycare to pick up Junior.

Mr. H appeared to be angry with me most of the time after I started working. He had sudden outburst that did not make sense. While I was in the middle of cooking dinner, he comes into the kitchen and asked me to hand him a glass out the dish rack. I was focus on taking my fried chicken out the skillet as I reached in the dish rack to grab a glass. Mr. H begin to yell that the glass has water on the outside. He tells me, if I ever hand him another glass with water on the outside, he will throw it on the floor with the food I am cooking for me to clean up. This was a side of Mr. H that I had never encounter. For the sake of peace, I did not reply to his outburst. After dinner while I was washing dishes, he begins to complain about the house not being as tidy as it was when I was not working. He goes off on me when I say to him, "maybe it is because you and your kids are home most of the day not cleaning up your mess." He goes off on me once again with the yelling. I was happy when Mr. H oldest daughter moved in with her boyfriend because she was pregnant and his youngest daughter hardly came home. This is what stop him from complaining about the house not being as tidy as when I did not work.

By the end of my second year of me working at Mitsubishi Electronics a co-worker went on an indefinitely medical leave of absence. The co-worker husband was ill which in turn caused my co-worker to provide full-time care to her husband. As our manager was interviewing replacements, we learned that the other co-worker had put in for a position in another department. Two new employees joined the department within three months of each other. I was promoted to a coordinator. Each coordinator was responsible for their own data entry.

Mitsubishi was starting to grow rapidly and needed to expand to add more office space as well as warehouse space. A third location was open on the same street as the two current locations. All were within walking distances. One year after the third location, my manager retired. Under the new manager, I was promoted to supervisor of the Order Control department. Five more employees were hire. There was a total of seven employees for me to supervise and I had been assigned the two largest distributors. Mr. H became extremely paranoid because of my promotion. He started stalking me at work by parking on the side street of the main building I worked in. Many times, I would have to walk paperwork over to the other two buildings. This would lead to an argument at home because Mr. H would demand to know why I went to the other buildings. Mr. H had become delusional in his fallacy's thoughts about my job. One morning Mr. H wakes me up an hour before my alarm clock goes off. He asked me to go in the garage with him to show me something. As I entered in the garage, he closes the garage door then he tells me to come into the area where the washer and dryer was located. I am thinking, "what is it that he needs to show me." Mr. H takes a handmade rubber whip attached to a wood handled from the shelf where the detergent is kept. He demanded me to tell him that I am having an affair at work and this is the reason I am going into the other two buildings at work. When I say to him, "how am

I having an affair when I come straight home from work without stopping anywhere other than to pick up Junior." Mr. H could care less about the truth. He kept threatening to beat me with the whip if I did not tell him that I was having an affair. Finally, I said what he wanted me to say. Mr. H started to cry then made me promise that I would end the affair and never do that to him again. I told him exactly what he wanted me to say. He hugged and kissed me before allowing me to go get ready for work. This was a huge red flag for me. I knew it was time to get out the house because this man has become deranged in his way of thinking.

I learned from this lesson that some people are put into our lives only for a season. Although I never loved Mr. H in a romantic way, I never disrespect him regards of what he thought in his mind, I never cheated on him, denied him of my body, nor neglect in keeping the household together. I paid all the bills in the house so that Mr. H could use his government assistance income on his kids. We used his food stamps to buy food. I never complaint about having to pay the bills. I did what was needed to keep the household functional. It was at this point in my life, I wonder if I could feel love for a man. I never felt what the other ladies would describe when they talked about their boyfriends or mate.

My mother had moved into a three bed-room house in Los Angeles near the airport. The house garage had been converted to a studio apartment. It had a full bathroom with two small rooms. Mr. H requested to always know my whereabouts. I needed a break from him, so I took my son Junior to go visit my mother at her new location. My mother shows me the studio apartment before asking me if I think my brother would rent it for $300 per month. I told her that I was not sure if he would want to live in a small place in the rear of her house. I was trying to buy some time for me to get up the nerves to tell my mom that I wanted to rent the studio. That weekend I tossed and turned in my sleep because I was wrestling with fear on asking my mom can I rent the place, and how I would safely move from Mr. H. house. That following Monday morning, I called my mother as I sat in my car at work before going into the building. As soon as my mother said hello, I blurted out my mouth, "mom, I would like for me and Junior to rent the studio apartment. I am having marital problems and need a safe place to live." I was surprised and happy when my mother said, "okay, when do you want to move in?" I told my mom I wanted to move in on Saturday morning and that I need one of my brothers to come help me move my clothes. My brother Big Al arrived at ten Saturday morning. Mr. H corner me in the closet as I was putting my clothes in large black plastic bags. He asked me what was I doing. I told him moving as I pulled away from him. He stood there with a shocked look on his face. He kept his temper under controlled in front of my brother. After loading my brother and my car with clothes, I put Mr. H key on the dining room table. I told him please do not come after me because I was not changing my decision to move. Once I was free from Mr. H house, I filed for divorce. Mr. H did not contest the divorce.

I was so grateful for the studio apartment and even more grateful it was separate from my mother's living space. I had privacy. My mother gave me a key to her house so I could use the washer and dryer. My mail was transferred to my mother's address since the studio was not a stand-alone address. I would pick up my mail every Sunday from my mom's place. I received a letter from the child-support division stating that I was ordered to pay fifty-two dollars a month in child support since the father was delinquent on the payments. I did not know they had contacted the father or should I say the rapist for child support. I could not remember telling them who the father was when I applied for government assistance. The next day at work, I called the contact person on the letter. I did not have a problem paying the child support. I wanted more information on how they found the father and why he did not pay. The contact person was very helpful; she explained to me that whenever a single mother applies for assistance she must interview with a child-support worker and a case worker. She stated that I told the child-support worker that I did not have any information about the father other than where he works and his name. She said, they were able to get the father home address from his employment records. She begins to voluntarily tell me all about the father. She tells me where he was currently working and that he had a lot of kids that he did not pay child-support for. I could not believe what I was hearing. It led me to wonder how many of those women did he rape. Also, I wonder if my son was his first child, but I did not ask her any questions about him. Where he worked was a short drive from where I was working. I could not believe it. I did not know what to do with this information. I was elated to hear that he did not deny my son was his child.

After a couple of months of paying the child-support that the rapist was supposed to be paying, I decided to let the rapist know that he did not break me. One day on my lunch break, I took two pictures of my son to the rapist job. I asked one of the employees if Mr. X was at work and available. When Mr. X came from the back to the front and saw me standing there, his eyes bucked wide open like he was seeing a ghost. I was very professional. I gave him the two pictures as I tell him that these are pictures of the son you refuse to pay child-support for. I turn around and walk out without saying anything else. I never seen my rapist again after that day. I paid child-support for about a year when they stop collecting it from me. I never called to question why they stopped.

Things were going well with me living in the studio apartment. One of my co-workers who worked in a different department at Mitsubishi Electronics had met a man who lived in Palmdale, which is approximately an hour drive from Los Angeles without traffic. Her and I was talking on the phone when she tells me that she is moving to Palmdale to live with this guy. I was in total shock because she only known the guy for a few months, less than six months. She had only been talking to me about this guy for one month, which made we question if she had just met this man a month ago. I tried to talk her out of it because she had two young daughter's around Junior age. That Saturday after I tried to convince her not to move, I was woken up, in the middle of the night, by mother calling me on the phone. My mom tells me that my friend with two little girls was at her door needing my help. Instantly without my mom saying her name, I knew who it was. I tell my mom to let her come through the house to the back. To this day, I do not know how my co-worker knew where I lived because I did not have any visitors over to my studio.

I call my co-worker Lady Bird. I met Lady Bird and her daughters who were in their pajamas at my mother's back door. The girls were carrying pillows and blankets. I was too tired to talk with Lady Bird about what happen. I told her that she and her girls had to squeeze in my son twin bed and we will talk in the morning. I put my son in my twin bed with me. Early the next morning Lady Bird takes her girls to her sister's house. Because I had a King Cab Nissan pickup truck, Lady Bird asked me if I could take her to get some of her items from Palmdale. I agree to help her get her clothes only. I asked my nephew to go with us. It took us over an hour to arrive at the location. Lady Bird and my nephew load the bed of my truck with as many boxes as they could fit. My nephew same a narrow spot for him to sit in the bed of the truck. After dropping off Lady Bird at her sister house and unloading the boxes into her sister's garage I was tired and ready to go home. It was around six in the evening. Lady Bird had the nerve to ask me if I could go back that evening to pick up another load of her items. I declined. The next day was Monday; my nephew and son had to go to school and neither of us had eaten dinner yet. Lady Bird did not come to work that next day on Monday.

Things were going well while living in the studio; however, it soon came to an end as Mr. H kept coming to my mother's house. He would park on the street and sit for hours spying on me. My mother asked him to stop but he would not. One Saturday night after returning home from the Company's Christmas party around 1pm in the morning, I was abruptly woken up by a big boom. Mr. H had kicked my door open while I was sleep. He thought I had a man inside with me. My mother was babysitting Junior. My mother got her gun and came to the back. Mr. H fast talked himself out of being shot. He promised my mother that he would come back during daylight hours to fix the door. I had to put a chair against the door to keep it closed. As promise, Mr. H came with a new door frame. He took the door off and repaired the frame. He made sure the door properly locked before leaving. I did not talk to him as he worked on the door. I refused to answer any of his questions. At that point I knew it was time to move.

Lady Bird was able to get another two bed-room, two bath apartment in the same building she had moved from when she moved in with a guy she had just met. This guy was married with a baby. This guy made the mistake of lying about his marriage status but not about where he lived. While him, his baby and wife was off visiting family, Lady Bird was moving into his house. She paid a locksmith to make a key to the kitchen door inside the garage. The locksmith believed Lady Bird was the owner because all her things were in the garage. When the homeowner came home with his family, Lady Bird was put out in the middle of the night with her girls. Because Lady Bird had racked up dealt with moving to and from Palmdale, she was looking for a roommate. I offered to become her roommate because I was looking to get away from Mr. H. A plus to becoming Lady Bird roommate is that she lives on the other side of town, in the city of Paramount which is approximately fifty minutes away from Mr. H. Another plus is Lady Bird had a huge master bedroom with a full bathroom. She moved her girls' bed in her bedroom. Me and my son shared a bedroom. I do not recall the amount of rent I paid, I know it was affordable and reasonable. After moving in with Lady Bird, I begin to save a little money each month. Immediately after moving in with Lady Bird, she begins to use my personal items, take my toilet paper and eat my food. Many days she would tell me to not come home early because her and her boyfriend needed some alone time. I was tired of hanging out at the mall trying to give her time with her boyfriend. One day I arrived home at eight that evening. I had food already cooked. I arrived home to empty pots. Lady Bird had given my dinner to her boyfriend who had the nerve to joke about him not understanding why I made cornbread to go with pot roast with green beans and white potatoes; yet, he ate it. I told myself to stay calm, I needed only two more months of saving money before I have enough money to move into my own place.

I had started talking to this guy at the job name Jay. He is a supervisor over one of the warehouses. We had been talking for months before we started dating. I did not want to tell Lady Bird that Jay and I was dating because she had told me that she had deep feelings for him. She said that she would fantasize about having sex with him. Also, she tells me that he declined her offer to give him sex. Jay had been asking to come to my home. I asked him to be patience as I was going to be looking for my own place soon. Lady Bird had informed me that her girls will be spending the weekend at their dad's house and that she will be spending the weekend with her man, the guy that ate my dinner. I decided to take advantage of the time alone by asking my sister to babysit on Saturday so that I could spend time with Jay. Jay and I was sitting close together having a drink as we watch TV, Lady Bird walks into the apartment to get more clothes. We all looked like we seen a ghost. Jay and I stared at Lady Bird without saying a word. Lady Bird said that she came to get a change of clothes. Lady Bird goes in her bedroom; she comes out in a sheer black sexy negligee. She looks Jay in his face and tells him, "This is what you have been missing out on Jay." I lost it, I cussed her out and proceeded to stand up from the couch when Jay held me back. He looked me in my eyes, as he says. "It is not worth it, hold onto your peace." Jay got up and left. Lady Bird tried to plea temporarily insanity declaring that she does not know what came over her and that she will never do anything like that to hurt me. She repeatedly tells me that she was sorry. I was happy when she left. I was so hurt. I did not know what to do or how to think. I cried myself to sleep. In my conversation to God, I asked him, why was there always some form of calamity in my life. What is it that I am doing wrong? I tell God that I want to change whatever it is that I am doing wrong. I asked God to please help me. I felt like God had gone silent on me. I was at a lost.

A month after this incident with Jay and Lady Bird, I found a one-bedroom apartment back in the city of Los Angeles. My relationship with Jay was short lived. One of Jay's co-workers who was also a supervisor in the warehouse told me that Jay was back with his ex-girlfriend. The co-worker said that Jay and his ex-girlfriend have an on again off again rocky relationship and the reason they are on again is because the girlfriend is pregnant. I immediately removed myself from becoming part of a love triangle. Jay never denied or confirmed what his co-worker had told me. Junior and I lived in our one-bedroom apartment in Los Angeles until the beginning of 1990. My sister had moved to Paramount. I decided to move closer to her because she would occasionally babysit Junior for me. I moved into a one-bedroom in the city of north Long Beach, which was a ten-minute drive to my sister's apartment in Paramount. After moving to Long Beach, my co-worker Diane introduces me to one of her husband's friends name Rod. Rod and I became close friends. We would talk for hours. Our relationship was not intimate. I never asked Rod if he had a girlfriend, however, I told him that I did not have a boyfriend. Rod was battling a court case; he ends up going to prison. We kept in touch mostly through writing each other with occasional collect calls from prison.

Rumors starts to spread at work that the company was having problems with its computer sales. A series of layoffs being to happen in small increments. The Order Control department was the last to be affected by the layoffs. I was not sure about my future with all the layoffs. Mitsubishi Electronics was my first professional job as an adult. I was feeling a little melancholy. A friend of mines, Ms. A, who use to be an employee I supervised invited me to attend family and friends' day at her church. The special service was on the first Sunday in September of 1990. I knew this would be a different experience for me. I was use to the protocol of the Catholic church. I was eager to experiment something different. The church service starts at Eleven; however, most people arrive around nine in the morning so that they could reserve seats in the front by laying clothes, bibles, and notes stating that the seat is taken. This was a new experience for me. After the early arrivals marked off their saved seats they would go and mingle. Because I rode in the car with my friend and other people, she knew that were members of the church I had missed eating breakfast to be on time. What I did not know is that these people stay all day at church. Unlike the Catholic church, the members of this church were very social before service starts. Once the praise team comes out to sing everyone run to their saved seats. I was amazed at the high energy everyone had. People were dancing, singing louder than the music and speaking in a foreign language. Some people would cry and rock back and forth while others dance in the isles. Compared to the Catholic church, this experience was very entertaining for me. People begin to calm down once the person who gives the announcements came to the podium. The preacher takes his seat in the middle of the announcements. Next, the preacher come to the podium to announce it is giving time. The deacons get in position with buckets in their hands. After giving time, the choir sings two songs before the preacher returns to the podium to preach. The amount of time all of this took place, prior to the preacher getting up to preach, in the Catholic church service would have been over.

The preacher sermon was very good. I was able to understand the message. The preaching technique in this church was more descriptive than in the Catholic church which helped me to understand the message with clarity. After the preacher ends his sermon, he called people up to the altar for prayer. With everything going on at work, I went up for prayer. As people was exiting church, I am thinking, "it is time to go eat." Boy, was I wrong. It was time for prayer upstairs. The two ladies in the car with me and my friend was part of a prayer warrior ministry at the church. Along with other altar workers they all gather to pray in what they called the upper room. At first, I was standing there watching them pray as I was thinking about food. One of the ladies who rode with me name Mrs. V begin to single me out and pray for me. She laid her hand on my forehead as she prayed. I begin to feel something that I could not explain. My body was reacting to what I was feeling by raising my hands and moving back and forth. The other prayer warriors saw what was happening and begin to join Mrs. V in praying for me. Mrs. V whisper in my ear, "Judy, God is calling you, he is waiting on you." I begin to cry. Mrs. V asked me if I believe Jesus Christ is the son of God and who is my Lord and Savior. I said yes. Then she asked if I repent for my sins and want to be baptized. I said yes. I was taken down stairs to the back of the church where two people changed their clothing to white linen. I had to change my clothing as well to white linen.

The male and female dressed in white linen begin to pray with me to be baptized of the holy spirit. To me it felt like hours they were praying with me. I begin to feel tire and hungry. The two praying with me begin to speak in tongues. At that time, I did not know it was called tongues. It was a foreign language to me. As they were speaking in tongues, I heard a voice that was not mines, speak into my mind telling me to mimic them. The voice said, if you mimic them, they would leave you along. I yelled at that voice that was talking in my mind. I said to it in my thoughts, "no, I want to know that this is real." Immediately after I said no, I felt something heavy, but not painful come into my body starting in my head and slowly moving down my body to my toes. I became very heavy in my spirit as I spoke in a very powerful strong foreign language. My voice felt very strong to me. People around me begin to praise God. I was taken to be the pool to be baptized of the water. When I came up from the water, I begin to speak in the powerful strong language again. I could not stop speaking in tongues for a while. Once I begin to calm down, I was able to change back into my clothes. Of course we stayed for the evening service that started at six. I got home that evening at nine. I had gone all day without food. I believe I ate a sandwich before going to bed. I do recall exactly what I ate. The next Sunday, I joined the church.

Shortly after joining church the Order Control department employees were being laid off two at a time. I did not have the fear or anxiety I had before being baptized.

By December of 1990, myself and my manager were the only two employees left in the department. We both was called into the VIP office. We each received severance pay and a computer. I waited until I was in my car to look at my severance pay check. It was in the amount of twenty thousand dollars. I could not believe I was given that much money and a computer. I lived on my severance pay for six months before looking for a new job. In June of 1991 I found a job working in the city of Wilmington as an accounting clerk. I worked for a hard wood lumber company. Furniture makers would buy the lumber.

Rod and I continued to be close friends while he was in prison. In August of 1991, Rod asked me to marry him. Yes, inmates can get marry while they are in prison. I say yes to Rod because he was a safe space to be in. After getting baptized, I was not interested in dating. I was tired of the ups and downs of relationships. I needed a break. Being marry to Rod gave me that break. Rod sent me three hundred dollars towards the cheap ring I bought just to show I was married. Rod and I got marry on October 25th of 1991. My marriage was my haven from men who was approaching me. Once I show my ring they would leave me along. Occasionally I would go visit Rod. Our communication continued to mainly be via phone or letters.

Shortly after marrying Rod, I received a phone call from a social worker. My mother gave the social worker my name and number as a possible candidate to foster my younger sister daughter who was in foster care. My younger sister always had trouble with drugs. Her son was removed from her home when he was around sixteen months. She would get high and leave him home alone. Also, she would be passed out in her apartment with the door open and her baby would be walking outside in a soil diaper and no shirt or shoes on. The neighbors got tire of having to save her son from harm. They called child protected service on her. Her son was removed from her home and placed in foster care. The worker was calling me about my sister third child Cherise. I was the one who gave Cherise her name. The foster mother who had Cherise since birth was an elderly woman who was in hospice care. According to the worker, Cherise had spent life living in her crib; therefore, she had problems with one foot turning inward as she walks. They were having trouble finding a home for Cherise. I explain to the worker that I worked full time and have my son to provide after school care for; therefore, I do not have the money to pay child-care for another child. The worker said that they would give me $345 dollars per month to care for Cherise and a yearly clothing allowance. Me knowing what it felt like to not have anyone help me with my son said yes, I will take her. Mrs. V from church lived five minutes away from me. She charged me $45 per week to babysit. I would take a daily amount of food for Cherise, prior to Mrs. V requesting me to bring a weekly large box of cream of wheat with her daily milk in bottles and daily jars of baby food. I knew the cream of wheat was probably for her family, but I was not going to complain. I was happy to have a babysitter.

A year after getting Cherise, the worker called me about my sister son DiAndre. The foster mother that had DiAndre was having trouble with him. Neighbors had witnessed the foster mother pushing DiAndre to the ground then putting her foot in his chest to hold him still. To not have her three other foster kids remove from her care, she had to have DiAndre removed from her care. I was not ready for this type of responsibility; however, it was difficult to say no to DiAndre and yes to Cherise. I welcome DiAndre back home to his family. I was living in a one-bedroom apartment when I got custody of Cherise and DiAndre. A two-bedroom was for rent in the same building I was living in. The manager allowed me to move in the two-bedroom apartment. The rent was slightly higher. I received $345 per month for DiAndre. I had to apply for a clothing allowance for DiAndre because the foster mother dropped him off with the clothes on his back, which was too small, and a bag with one change in underwear that was too large and one oversized sweater. He had no other clothes. His sneakers had holes in them. I had to take off work because I could not enroll him in school until I received the proper paperwork from the worker as well as the voucher to purchase him new clothes.

I was now in the foster care system as the person who will take my sister kids. Many days I sat thinking about what it was about me that separated me from my family. I knew in my heart that I did not do anything to be cast out other than love with all my heart and I show my love in my actions. I realized that the darkness in people including family dislike the light in people who is good hearted. I am caring and good hearted. I refuse to make apologies for who I am. I do not want to change to match the dark energy I am receiving from people who envy the light that is in me. It is not about self-boasting; it is about recognizing the God that is in me and with me. I will never deny God to please the darkness in people.

Once again, I was approached by the social worker because my sister five mouth old daughter needed to be replaced because her foster mother was moving out of town to Georgia. I told the worker that I need to pray about it. I was complexed and not sure what to do. I got on my knees and begin to cry out to God. I cried out, "Lord, I need you now, I do not know what to do. My heart is aching; my mind is confused. Lord, I did not place my special need child to take in my sister's kids. When is enough, enough. My sister cannot keep having babies for me to take. God when do my family provide me with support. God allow your light to guide my footsteps by luminating the path without confusion. Let my heart know the right thing to do according to your will. In the name of your son and my savior Jesus Christ I pray, Amen." Two days after praying this prayer the foster mom called me. We talked for about thirty minutes before we scheduled a time to meet. In my heart I instantly knew what I needed to do. I quit my job and applied for government assistance for myself and my son. I was still getting $345 dollars per month for each of my sister's kids. At seven months, my sister baby Lenise was placed in my home. Shortly after receiving Lenise, I learned that my sister was ill and was on dialysis. The lifetime of drug use has weakened her bones. She was no longer able to carry a child in her womb. After receiving Lenise I moved a half of mile away into a three-bedroom with two full baths apartment. I became a full-time mom of four.

DiAndre had fear that the workers would remove him from his family. He was enjoying being with his sisters and seeing his family including his birth mom. I told him that I was going to adopt them so that he could focus on being a kid and not worrying about grown people problems. I kept the boys busy with sports at the local park and with school. Once Lenise turned two years old, I enrolled in Cerritos community college. The college had a program for low-income mothers to registered their kids in daycare for the hours the parent was in class. I was able to drop the girls off before attending class and pick them up after my last class. Rod started to complaint when I decided to legally adopt my sister kids. Going to school and raising four kids put a strained on my marriage. I was too busy to visit, and no longer could afford the collect calls. In November of 1996, I filed for divorce. Our divorce was finalized in March of 1997. I went years without dating. The kids and church were my life and finally I was happy and at peace.

I became very active in church after quitting my job to care for the kid's full time. I joined the adult usher board.

Once I became an usher, my friend, Ms. A, who originally invited me to the church, joined the usher board as well. Ms. A was already a member of one of the three choirs at church. I considered Ms. A, a very close friend. When I was her supervisor at Mitsubishi Electronic, we would help each other with our kids. I would often invite her and her boys to my home for dinner. We were like sisters. Our kid's relationship were very close; they would tell people that they were cousins.

Having to no longer focus on the needs of a husband, I was able to redirect that attention to my spiritual growth. Every day after dinner I would go in my room and spend time with God. I would read and study my bible, pray and tell God my dreams, concerns, fears, disappointments, and the enjoyment of my day. I would thank God for his daily blessings. I became more spiritually intuitive or should I say more aware of my spiritual intuitiveness. I recalled visiting my friend Yvonne in northern California. Yvonne and I became friends through our husbands. Because of the long drive, I stayed overnight at her house. That evening, Yvonne and I was sitting at the dining room table talking when she received a phone call from a church member. Yvonne was telling the person on the phone about this dream she had.

She expressed to the friend that she could not shake this dream from her thoughts. As Yvonne describe what happen in her dream, I could see the meaning of the dream in details of the description. Immediately after Yvonne ends her call, I tells her that I know what her dream means. This was the first time I ever interpret someone's dream. Yvonne stared at me in silence as I gave her the interpretation. When I finished, she picks up her phone to call the same person she was talking to on the phone in my presence. She tells this person, "You have no idea who I have in my house right now." She continued to say, "I have a prophetess in my house who can interpret dreams." After Yvonne end her phone call for the second time, her and I begin to talk about the interpretation. I tell Yvonne that I do not see myself as a prophetess. I say to her, that I have insight on somethings that I cannot explain why I have this insight. My insight is not all the time. It is something that happen periodically. I cannot turn it on or off or control when it happens. Yvonne tells me that the interpretation was regarding something that she had not talk to anyone but God about. At that moment I was happy that God had used me to bring confirmation and clarity to Yvonne.

I had been a member of my church for approximately five years when the preacher died. Within a couple of days of hearing about the preacher's death, he came to me in a dream that felt real. The preacher was clothed in a white robe trimmed in gold. He was wearing a white cloth crown that was shaped liked a pyramid with a point at the top. The preacher took me in the spirit realm to a high school gymnasium where basketball would be played. Sitting on the bleachers was the church choir. It was the choir that my close friend Ms. A joined. Ms. A was on the first row sitting next to a husband-and-wife choir member. The wife was between Ms. A and her husband. Ms. A was talking to the wife about me in a very negative way. She was defaming my character with lies and telling personal business of mines. The husband and wife were hysterically laughing. At that moment of me being presence in the spirit realm, I felt sad at what I was witnessing. Sensing my sadness, the preacher, who we all call Bishop, looked at me, and told me to sing. I replied, "Bishop, I cannot sing." "Sing, Sing," shouted Bishop in a powerful but not scary voice. I begin to sing. To my amazement, I was singing with the most powerful beautiful sounding voice. My singing woke me up from the dream to find that I was singing in real time in my sleep. I could hear it as I woke up. I was not sure what the dream meant at that time. God revealed it much later.

Somehow, it was spread around the church that I had the Daniel gift of interpreting dreams. I never told anyone other than Ms. A what happen when I visit Yvonne. I believe Ms. A was trying to embarrass me and shame my character by telling someone in the church what happen at Yvonne house. She probably was looking to get laughter from telling. I believe whoever she told did respond the way Ms. A was hoping they would; instead, people in the church begin to approach me about interpreting their dreams. I felt uncomfortable at first giving people the interpretation of their dreams, but as I witness people crying and asking me how did I know what I told them. It made me have compassion for God's people. I thought about the times I use to daydream about having a two-way conversation with God and he would immediately reply. People would offer to give me money to interpret their dreams. I refused to take it. I would always decline. Taking money did not feel right in my spirit. Sometimes, people would use someone else to pass an envelope to me with money in it. It was never a lot of money. It was usually between three to twenty dollars.

There were times I kept the money other times I would put it in the offering plate at church.

I interpret dreams for years. People would call me from other states. They would tell me that someone in the church gave them my phone number. Church member would call me in the middle of the night and early in the morning before my alarm would go off for me to get my kids up. When I return to work, people would call me on my job. It was beginning to be over whelming. I begin to cry out to God that it was too much. I needed rest. I wanted to help people but it was too much. Sometimes I would pick up spirits from people. I had to constantly cleanse my house and anoint myself with blessed oil. A church member came to my house once, and when she left, the dark spirit that was attached to her stayed in my house. I was sitting in my living room when I saw in my peripheral vision a three feet dark image run from one room of my house into another room. After seeing the dark image, that night while I was sleep in bed, I turn on my stomach. I had not slept on my stomach since I was a young kid. The dark spirit hops on my back. I could not open my eyes or talk while the weight of this spirit was on my back. I got so mad in my spirit to the point that I yelled within my spirit saying "Get off me now! In the name of

Jesus, get off me now!" My voice was strong and powerful. The dark image jumped off me. My eyes open and I was able to talk. I got up out of bed and told that spirit to get out my house, and that it was not welcome into my home and that in the powerful name of Jesus I have command over you. Also, I said to that dark spirit, the bleed of Jesus was over my door post; and I command you in the name of Jesus to go back to the pits of hell where you came from. I went to open my front door and repeated what I previously said to the dark spirit. As I closed my door, I tell the spirit to never come back ever.

After the incident with the dark spirit, I interpret dreams for another three years. Once again, I cried out to God, asking him to allow me to retire because I was tired. I received the peace from God to retired; however, he still used me to give message to people. When God tells me to give a message, my spirit has an unrest until the message has been given to the person. Delivering a message is much lighter than interpreting dreams.

Ms. A, hidden agenda to defame my character was slowly being revealed. People in the church would notice it and warn me. She intentionally became close to the usher board director so that she could convince him to appoint her as his secretary. Once she was appointed as the secretary, she convinced the director to set a bylaw stating that the usher board presidents could not serve more than two years. There was a total of four different usher boards at the church with a different president over each board. I was appointed president over the senior usher board although I was not a senior. I was president of the senior board for approximately a year when the bylaw was implemented. The other three presidents had worked for years as the president over their assigned usher board. I received notice from the director secretary that I was being sat down and replaced by someone else. The president over the adult usher board, this was the board I originally joined, was also sat down and replaced by someone else. The other two presidents were allowed to remain president over the boards regardless of the many numbers of years they served as president. This was clearly a hater move by Ms. A.

Haters are the people who tries to dim your light because your job well done is being recognized and honor and because people like who you are as a person. Haters act in the same image as Cain did in the bible when he killed his brother Abel because he was jealous that Abel found favor in God eyes. Just like Cain was the first born of Adam and Eve,

Ms. A was a member of the church first when she invited me to attend. As a choir member, she joined the usher board because I had joined. Because of my faithfulness and service as an usher was recognized by people, Ms. A became jealous. Just like Cain, she sought out to kill, steal, and destroy me. As it is written in the bible in Genesis chapter four verse seven: "If you do well, will you not be accepted? And if you do not do well, sin lies at the door. And its desire is for you, but you should rule over it." God spoke this to Cain. Cain chose the latter which is to allow sin to rule him rather than him rule over sin. Ms. A did the same. Ms. A did not stop here with her quest to kill, steal, and destroy me. More will be revealed in this book.

After graduating from Cerritos college with an Associate of Art degree in Business Accounting, I was ready to go back to work. By this time the boys were in high school and the girls were in elementary. Following my normal pattern when searching for a job, I went to a staffing agency. I accepted a temp position at Federal Warranty Service Corp located in Buena Park. I worked as an accounting clerk. My position mainly handled receivables; however, many times I had to assistant with payables. Once again, I was hired as a full-time permanent employee after three months. As I was approaching my one-year anniversary I find out that the company was closing its California location. A few employees were offered a position in the corporate office located in Atlanta, Georgia. Many employees were told if they remain at the company until it closes, they will receive a very generous severance pay. Well, it did not take a rocket scientist to tell me that I had nothing coming with only one year of employment at the company, except a layoff notice. I started to secretly look for another job.

I found a job in Anaheim Hills at Transitional Technology as an accounting clerk. Transitional Technology was a small company. Although I was hire as a full-time permanent employee, once again my stay was short-term. The company owner's son hired me against the will of the father. I was the only employee who did not speak Spanish. The company's dynamic mainly consists of men. There were only three women employees. The owner replaced his son as the manager of the accounting department. The son still worked at the company in another position. The new manager wasted no time promoting the Spanish speaking receptionist to accounting clerk. My job was to trained the promoted clerk. I knew at this point I was being fired. I decided to stay until I was fired. A few months later I was called into the new accounting manager office. I walked in, sat down, looked the manager in the eyes then said, "are you going to give me any paperwork that states I am fired or laid-off?" He looked at the supervisor for a moment than says "yes" to me. My reply was, "let us not prolong this with a speech, I am ready to go home." He hunched his shoulders before passing me the papers. I said, "thank you," before grabbing my purse and leaving the building. I felt relieved and peaceful.

I applied for unemployment and was approved. Unemployment sent me a letter in the mail about a special program they have in preparing recipient for their next job. According to the letter, unemployment would pay for me to take a trade course during the twenty-six weeks I qualify for unemployment. The paper stated that I would not have to search for a job while attending the course. I immediately enrolled in the trade school authorized by unemployment. The trade school was thirty minutes away from my house. The school hours were eight to five Mondays through Fridays. To get my check from unemployment the school had to sign the time sheets I mailed to the unemployment office for payment. No excuses, I had to show up daily and complete each course to get my check. The trade school taught medical billing. The last month of the trade school was finding a job. Each student had to search during school hours for a job and apply for the job while at school. Also, the students had to submit an up dated resume to the school office. The school would fax resumes to jobs without the knowledge of the students. I received an interview with Marina Medical Billing located in Garden Grove. The school had fax them my resume. The interview went well. I was offered a job in the accounting department as an accounts receivable clerk. I accepted the position.

My new job started the last week in September of 1999. I loved working at Marina Medical Billing. The accounting department applied patients' payments all day. Each clerk was assigned different hospital's emergency room payments from patients to apply in the system. Because of traffic my commute to work was forty-five minutes to an hour. The company moved in 2002 to Cerritos which was only a fifteen to twenty-minute surface street drive from my home. Because the job was closer to me, I was able to take night courses at the University of Phoenix off campus location in Long Beach. I had to drive to Garden Grove for a couple of courses that was not offer at the off campus. I received a Bachelor of Science degree in Business

Management. After graduating, my manager at Marina suggested that I apply for the Credentialing Manager position. I did not want to be the manager over a department I knew nothing about. I was talked into taking the position. Many of the managers opposed me getting the position. Not only did I not like the position, I had to deal with managers spying on me. Withholding information from me. Searching through my office before and after I leave work. And questioning everything I did; although, I did my job correctly. I found another job in La Mirada at Dale Tiffany as an Accounts Receivable Specialist. The Friday before starting my new job, I went to work at Marina early in the morning before the normal staff arrived. I put my letter of resignation on my desk. I took all my personal belongings and left before anyone could see me. The Human Resources' manager kept calling me to come back. I did not pick up her calls. They even offer to give me back my old position. I refused to take their calls to say I declined returning to my old position.

In March of 2005 Dale Tiffany welcome me with open arms. I was amazed to find out that Dale Tiffany is the makers of the Tiffany lamps sold mainly at JC Pennys. The company was small but powerful in the sales of the Tiffany lamps. There were less than twenty-five employees who ran the office. I do not know how many employees worked in the warehouse. I never seen more than ten. To always have an employee in the office, I agree to take the one to two lunch breaks with one other person. Everyone else went to lunch from noon to one. One day, while everyone was at lunch, the other person who took lunch the same as I came to me with a statement that blew my mind. She says to me, "Judy, you interpret dreams." I looked at her with my mouth open because I was in shock. She was a Filipino lady who were a couple of years older than myself. I say to her, "how do you know I interpret dream? I never tell people that I interpret dreams, so how do you know that?" She says to me, "let this be the validation that you need to know what you are doing is real." She then asked me to interpret a dream for her. I was more than happy to interpret her dream. Her and I became very close. She was the person who told me that three employees in the office had applied for jobs at a new company in the area, and she was one of them. She explained to me that the owner of the company did not believe in giving rises every year and that they had worked for years without any pay increase. After working at the company for six months the owner called me to his office to interview me. I did not understand why. He did not fire me after he interviewed me; however, it made me feel uncomfortable like I was being watched. I begin to look for another job as well. I did not want to be left behind feeling uncomfortable and watched. At the end of December 2005 before Christmas, I got an interview at Daylight Transport in Long Beach. A week after the interview at Daylight, I received a letter from them stating that they gave the position to someone else. I was extremely surprised when I received a call from Daylight's HR person on January 5th, 2006 to come for an Excel test for the position of Accounts Payable Specialist. I was told if I pass the test, the position is mines. I took the test the next day on the 6th. I got ninety-seven on the test. The manager and Director came in the HR office to congratulate me and welcome me to the company. I was given my hours and pay rate in that visit. They asked me when did I want to start. I told them that I wanted to give my current employer a one week notice and that I could start on January 16th, 2006.

I worked at Daylight Transport for sixteen years. I was the only person who handled payables for seven locations. I was responsible for all money paid out as well as for the driver's pay. Periodically someone would help with entering request for claims and refunds. For the most part, I enjoyed my job. As the company begin to grow, adding new locations and testing the system with new location, I begin to feel under appreciated. I begin to constantly complaint that I needed help. Every department was getting new employees to accommodate for the growth in the company, except the Accounts Payable department which was me. The Accounts Payable department had three accountants, two people applying receivables payments, and two people working receivable adjustments, and one person, myself handing payables. During Covid, I had to learn a new financial system because we were changing from the old system to a new one. I had to test the new system in every area of payables. The banking system was new; therefore, I had to process payables differently. I had seven locations calling me for payment status of their bills. I had vendors calling me for updated payment status. I was at a breaking point; yet I voice was not being heard. An employee who returned to work from maturity leave was assigned to help me. This employed came back on a Monday before the 4th of July on that coming Saturday. This employee put in for vacation on that Friday before the 4th and that Monday after the 4th. She works the rest of July only to go back on a medical leave of absence. I was not frustrated with the employee; I was frustrated with management for not getting me proper help.

My manager tells me the employee would only be out for a month. When I spoke with the employee, wishing her a speedy recovery, I say to her I will see you in a month. The employee reply was, "is that what our boss told you." I said "yes." The employee became silent. Her silence spoke loud and clear to me. I told myself if this employee does not come back after one month I am quitting. I gave the company two months to see if the employee was returning soon. When my manager had no reply for me, I submitted a two-week resignation letter to HR with a copy of my resignation to the Director and Chief Financial Officer. I was asked by the Director to give a copy to my manager. My manager asked me if I could stay for three more months while she looks for help. I declined. Because no one knew how to do my job, I allowed them to video record me for my last two weeks so that they could use the video recordings to train the new person.

Many personal things happen within the sixteen years I was employed at Daylight Transport. My sons graduated high school and moved out the home. My birth son moved in with his dad and my adopted son moved in with his birth mother, my sister. My oldest adopted daughter Cherise finished her last year of school in Job Corp, due to her not applying herself in school. At the age of fifteen, Cherise lost her focus in school. She was very smart in all subjects except math. She would normally complete her assignments ahead of the class. I could not understand what changed in her life to cause her to no longer focus on her class work. She was in threat of not graduating from high school because she would sit in class and do nothing. The school counselor felt maybe continuation school would be better for Cherise. I felt Job Corp would be better for her because of the structural setup. The students live on campus and are required to complete a trade and all courses in attaining a high school diploma within two years. Cherise selects a trade in culinary art. She would work on her trade but not on completing the courses in attaining a high school diploma. The counselor at Job Corp stated that Cherise was wasting their time and her time by not applying herself. They decided to remove her from the trade so that she would have to focus on completing her courses.

Ms. A contacted me to ask me if I was going to attend Cherise graduation. I did not know there was going to be a graduation. The only information I received from the counselor was that Cherise had finally finished her courses and would be leaving Job Corp a year ahead of schedule with an incomplete because she was withdrawn from her trade. I was happy to hear from the counselor that Cherise was getting a high school diploma. I did not ask him about a graduation. Ms. A tells me that she knows it is a short notice for me to have someone cover for me at work, for this reason she had already taken Cherise to the mall and bought her a dress and that herself and her mom and son will be attending Cherise graduation. My thoughts are racing now because I am thinking, why am I just now hearing about this and why Ms. A did not tell me before buying Cherise a dress. Ms. A assures me that she would take pictures at the graduation for me. A couple of days after the graduation Ms. A sends me pictures of Cherise in her cap and gown. After seeing the dress Cherise was wearing I was happy a gown covers up the inappropriate dress. She had on a mini halter top dress without a bra. I could not believe Ms. A had my daughter looking like a street walker. I later find out that Ms. A had been secretly picking up Cherise on Friday evenings from Job Corp to stay at her house and would take her back on Sunday evenings. I knew that Job Corp allowed the students to go home on the weekends; however, Cherise would tell me that she wanted to stay at Job Corp on weekends with her friends. I did not know the magnitude of influence Ms. A had on my three adopted kids until much later when her plot to destroy me affected the kids in a devastating way. As a parent we must cover our kids in prayer because our eyes will not be on them twenty-four hours of each day policing their every move. Our good intentions of teaching our kids morals and values can be disrupted by the influences of people like Ms. A. We parents must trust the process of training up a child in the way they should go, with the hope, should they be led or influence contrarily, they would one day return because the morals and values did not depart from them.

Cherise enrolled in Cerritos Community College when she was seventeen. She was too young and immature in taking the responsibility in the role of a college student serious. She sat in class basically to get a financial aid check. She never took notes; never did any homework, and she fail every test. She had to learned through trial and error that the government was not handing out financial aid to people who fail their course regardless of them attending class. While attending Cerritos College, Cherise attended a meeting held by army recruiters. They sold her on the amount of pay she would get monthly once she enlisted in the army. The recruiters stayed in contact with Cherise for the two months wait in her turning eighteen. I did my best in explaining to Cherise that the army was no joke and what it entails. She decided to enlisted anyway.

After Cherise enlisted in the army, my youngest adopted daughter Lenise begin to follow in her birth mom's footsteps with school. She was kicked out of regular school and continuation school. She begins to hang around a group of girls who was all about the street life. Her attitude and association with her new friends resulted in her serving time in juvenile hall. At age seventeen, Lenise left home and ran the streets. The probation department was looking for her; however, her friends hid her well out of anyone's sight. Lenise returns home at age eighteen pregnant with her first child. After giving birth to her son, she moves in with the father of her child. Three beautiful kids later, Lenise is still living with the father of her kids.

Life lessons can strengthen a person or break them. I watched life lessons break people in unrecognizable horrific ways in my community and in my family. I endure a great deal of pain at the hands of my family. I spent my life trying to understand the role I had in warrantying the treatment I received from my family. It was difficult for me to accept that family could be so heartless to someone they supposed to love. If they did not love me; why. I needed to see what I did wrong that separate me from their love and grace. Because of who God is to me, I refused to allow the horrific life lessons I received to break me. Also, because of who God is to me, I refused to match my family dark energy that they so freely give to me. Matching their energy, in my eyes, would separate me from God. I know I am not perfect, but one thing I strive to live by is, to give and do unto others what it is that I want God to give to me. I need God to survive. Therefore, how could I give hate and expect love from God.

I fight daily in my mind to keep my natural and spiritual eyes on God. My natural eyes look at the power in God's creation here on earth, starting with myself when I look in the mirror. Also, when I heard the powerful sound of thunder, the boisterous wind and how it all obeys God voice. It helps me to see his power. I love the beauty in God's creation of nature. These beautiful creations are the evidence of who is God. In faith I believe the words of the bible that God is love, light, the great I AM, and my creator. I believe that God is not a liar and that his word cannot return to him void; therefore, I believe when Jesus said to his disciples in Matthew chapter 17, verse 20 "I say to you, if you have faith as a mustard seed, you will say to this mountain, move from here to there and it will move; and nothing will be impossible for you." My belief God is greater than the pain I receive from life lessons that causes calamity. I believe God uses life lessons to strengthen. I always ask God what is the lesson I need to gain from this pain; from this calamity. I want the lesson to be made clear so I could grow and move pass the calamity of the lesson.

I must admit, when my mom gave the social worker my phone number as a candidate to foster my sister's kids, I was angry with her. My family has always depended on me to bail them out or assist them in one way or another; yet, they were never willing to assist me. A couple of times at the requested of my mother, I received help from the one brother who never gave me any problems. His street name is Big Al. He always stayed to himself away from family drama and confusion. Looking back, I never recall him and I having any type of disagreement or argument. He was a street dude; therefore, he was never at home. He was the brother who came with my mother in the middle of the night when someone broke into my one-bedroom apartment. He was the one who help me move safely from my first husband's house. Big Al is eighteen months younger than the brother I call "The Thief."

When I foster and later adopted my sister kids, my brothers, The Thief, became angry at me because the kids called me mom. He tried to persuade the kids to call me auntie Judy. Because the kids refused to call me auntie Judy, my brothers, The Thief and Bow, verbally abused me by saying that I threw away my birth son and stole my sister's kids. My sister was okay with the kids calling me mom. She preferred the kids to call her by her government name. There were no issues between my sister and I after I adopted her kids. She was happy I took her kids out of the foster care system.

My brothers, The Thief and Bow team up to attack me verbally; yet, when our oldest brother committed suicide, I was the one who comfort them. After serving eight years in the army my oldest brother lived in Florida with his wife and son. He used recreational drugs to numb the physical pain from being shot and emotional pain. Because my brother was estranged from his wife due to his use of drug, the state Coroner called my mother to help in the decisions for my brother burial. Again, my mother redirects the caller by giving them my phone number. The coroner informed me that they had my brother military information and would make sure my brother was bury in a veteran cemetery and that their purpose in calling was to give the family rights in the burial process. I worked remotely with the female coroner. After my brother was bury, she mailed me the location of the cemetery and location of his plot. The Thief would call me in the middle of the night crying. He had daily nightmares about our older brother shooting himself in the mouth with a shot gun. I would have to calm The Thief with words of peace, comfort, joy, and hope, and from blaming himself because of the last conversation he had with our brother. Because our older brother had called The Thief for money to buy drugs shortly before committing suicide, The Thief called our brother a lot of derogatory names. The Thief guilt was causing his nightmares. As much as I dislike my brothers, The Thief and Bow, I do love them and do not want to see them hurting. I did not want another suicide in my family. This is the reason I took the time to talk life and peace into my brother spirit each night.

When my sister, the birth mother of my adopted kids, pass away, my mother asked me and my baby brother Bow to assist her at the mortuary. Because of my sister's lifestyle, for years my mother had life insurance on her. At the mortuary, I saw my mother in a way I had never witness before. My mother carefully picked out the best and most expensive casket and other accessories. After the mortuary director calculated the total due, there was five thousand left over from the insurance check. My mother shows the director the insurance check. She tells him that the total will be paid in full in two days after the bank clears the check. My brother Bow tells my mom to sign the check over to him so that he can deposit it in his bank and could take care of getting the payment to the director. She then tells him to take one thousand for himself, and to give each of my sister kids a thousand and to give me a thousand. I tell my mom that I did not want any money. I told mom after my brother takes his thousand to give the balance of four thousand to my sister's birth kids. The kids were grown with their own bank accounts. Instead of my brother Bow following my mom instructions, he kept the entire balance of five thousand for himself. Once things had settled from the funeral, I told my mom that my brother did not follow her wishes in giving the kids their money. She told me to talk to Bow because she did not want to argue over death money. I decided to let it go as well.

By the time I turn fifty-three, the kids were out the house. I could redirect my attention to self. After I divorced my second husband Rod, I had not dated anyone. All my time and attention went towards the kids, church, and work. As I refocus my life on self, it brought back up issues I had swept under the rug. The issues from being rape was lying dormant. The thought of dating and trusting someone was scary to me. In my mind, I decided to be single for the rest of my life. The thought of being single allowed me the freedom to be me. I cut the perm from my hair leaving the new growth to define the length of my hair. I wore my natural curly short hair. During this transitional period of my life, I would go to the movies and out to eat alone. I was at peace with self. I had put some things in a small public storage. Over the years, I had collected a lot of pictures of the kids growing up as well as memorabilia. Included was all my oldies music in the form of cassette tapes, cd's, eight tracks as well as beta and VHS movie tapes. I had approximately five tubs full of photos. The kids and I was always busy and taking pictures. I asked my brother, The Thief, to help me carry tubs to my car for storage. He assured me that I did not have to pay storage because he had a loft in his garage that I could use to store my belongs. I was hesitating at first, but saving the monthly storage is what persuaded me. My thoughts were what harm can he do to pictures and old tapes. The harm was later learned.

Now that my household has downsized because the kids are living independent lives. I rented a small apartment just for one. Many times, after work I would stop at the store on the way home for an item or two. One day I decided to go to a store pass where I lived. I do not recall why I chose to drive three miles farther away from my home. Anyhow, I am in the produce area of the store carefully inspecting the fruits and vegetables I want to purchase when this guy walks near me and begin to stare nonstop. I felt his eyes on me, which caused me to look up from the produce. He gave me a huge smile that lasted at least a minute. My thoughts were, does he know me. Why is he not saying anything, just staring. After, I looked up, he continued to stare for a few seconds before walking away. I thought to myself, that was strange. It was like he suddenly disappeared. I continued to do my shopping not thinking anymore about it. Ten minutes later at the opposite end of the store, I ran into the same guy again. This time he starts walking towards me. I stopped to look at an item on the shelf while looking at him with my peripheral vision. He walks up to me and grabs my attention with "hello." I turn in his direction and replied with "hello." He asked me what island I was from. I looked confused and said, "excuse me; what do you mean what island I am from." Then he asked, "are you Caribbean." I replied, "no, I was born and raised in the USA. He asked me if he could call me sometimes. My initial thought was "no" before my thoughts switched to me thinking, "what is wrong with having a friend, nothing serious, just a friend;" therefore, I replied with yes. We exchanged phone numbers and names.

His name is Calvin; he called me very day around 7pm. We would talk for fifteen to twenty minutes each evening. After a month of talking on the phone, Calvin asked me out on a date. We went to a movie and dinner. Of course, his representative personality was a perfect pleasant gentleman. Calvin and I spent every weekend together; many times, either going to the movies or out to eat, sometimes both on the same day. Calvin would always pay and drive. Occasionally I would invite him to my apartment for dinner and to watch a movie on DVD. After six months of dating and talking on the phone every day, Calvin asked me to marry him. I told Calvin that I needed to think about it; because, I had promised myself that I would be single for the rest of my life. Calvin gave me the space to think about it by not asking me again until I was ready to talk about it.

Self-reasoning about marriage helped me to weigh the pros against the cons in my last two marriages. I started by looking at the common denominator in my last two marriages. In both marriages I was not in love with either husband, nor did they give me that feeling of butterflies in my gut. Both were a help to me in some form. These were the only pros that came to mind. In both marriages the cons were the same; I was the financial provider. Both ex-husbands wanted to control and isolate me from family and friends which lead to the demise of our marriage. I could clearly see the common denominator in both marriages being carry over into the new relationship. However, in comparison to the ex-marriages the common denominators in the new relationship would be both a pro and a con rather than a pro or a con. Calvin form of help, in the relationship, is that he financially can handle more than fifty percent of the expenses. He appears to be okay with the relationships I have with family and friends. I was concern if his pleasant gentleman personality was only a representative of his true self; and if it is, this means he would not be the same person after marriage. I decided to take a chance in marrying Calvin.

As previously stated, many personal things happen within the sixteen years I was employed at Daylight Transport. I had been working at Daylight Transport close to eight years when I married Calvin. After marrying Calvin I begin to believe I have this invisible magnet that draws to me the same type of men. A week before marrying Calvin, I moved into his apartment with him. He was living in a two-bedroom, two bath apartment. He stated it was the only available apartment in the building where he wanted to live. I used the spare bedroom as my dressing room. We had his and hers bathrooms, which made getting ready for work in the morning a smooth process. A couple of weeks after I got marry, my messy co-worker asked me for my phone number, she stated that she wanted to talk with me in private about something personal. I gave her my cell phone number. A weird thing happens the evening that Sandra called me. Immediately after saying "Hello Sandra," Calvin goes into his bathroom with the door open and begins to talk out loud to himself. He was saying so many cuss words as he spoke about some guys on his job who made him angry. He was talking like these guys were standing in front of him. His voice was projecting like he was speaking in front of a microphone. I tried to ignore it by raising my voice on the phone with Sandra. It was not working. I told Sandra that I need to end our phone conversation and that I will talk to her another time. I was so embarrassed to face Sandra the next day at work. I apologized to Sandra for the way Calvin was talking. I told her that he was talking to his co-workers who had upset him. Sandra's reply to me was, "I thought I might have to call the police, but then I realized I did not know your address. Calvin only reply to his behavior was "I am sorry." I am sorry does not bring clarity to a mental break down. I realized at that moment, marriage number three might be worse than the other two.

My oldest son was the only child of mines who met Calvin before getting marry. I did not know my daughter Cherise was medically discharged from the army after serving six of the enlisted eight years. She received twenty-thousand dollar in pay upon her discharged. Also, she moves in with Ms. A after being discharged. She lived with Ms. A for a few months before getting her own place. My older sister had to buy Cherise a bed after she moved into her own place, which led me to wonder what happen to her money. I do not believe in parenting a grown child; especially one who is living independently and who has served our country. I will give advice is asked. At times I will suggest something; however, I will not tell my grown kids how to live their lives.

After finding out that Cherise was discharged, I invited her and my youngest daughter Lenise to dinner so that they could meet my new husband. Both girls loved my spaghetti with grounded turkey and turkey sausage. I made a salad and baked some garlic bread. I do not recall what we had for dessert. I got marry in December, and the girls came to dinner the first Saturday in February. It was a cold rainy evening in Southern California. I was happy they did not cancel due to the weather. Lenise arrived dress appropriate for the weather. Living with Ms. A, Cherise gave me a flashback to her graduation dress that Ms. A had bought for her. She came to dinner dress in what I call booty shorts. Some people call them Daisy Dukes. These shorts are so short that if you slightly bend over your butt cheeks will show. She was wearing a mid-rip blouse. She did not have on a jacket. I immediately went into mommy mode and asked her where is her clothes. I could not believe she came outside in the winter dress like she was going to the beach. Lenise laughs as she shook her head and hutch her shoulders. Cherise did not answer me. She comments about the food smelling good. We all ate dinner, had good conversation and watched a movie.

Lenise asked for some personal paperwork I had of hers in my safe. Us three, myself, Lenise, and Cherise went into the spare bedroom to go through the paperwork in my safe. Cherise left out the bedroom for approximately ten minutes as Lenise and I was talking as I search through the paperwork. Cherise returns with a smirk look on her face. It

caught my attention; however, I did not ask her about it.
After finding Lenise paperwork, the girls left because it was
getting late and they both had far to drive. As I was cleaning
the kitchen and putting away the leftover food, Calvin comes
into the kitchen to express his disapproval of Cherise actions
when Lenise and I was in the bedroom. He tells me that
Cherise came into the living room while he was sitting in his
recliner watching TV. She stands in front of him to block the
television. She then says to him, "what are you doing in here
all along looking spoil." Calvin tells me that he recognized
that spirit and decided to be quiet and not say anything to
her. He tells me she stood there in front of him for a few
minutes waiting on him to say something; but he remained
silent. I believe him. I am sensitive to spirits and Cherise's
spirit has been different after her and Ms. A have become
close friends. Of course, Cherise denied what Calvin told me.
I decided to be more observant of Cherise actions whenever
she comes to my home.

Calvin soon felt into the same habits of my last two
husbands. He wanted to control me and isolate me from my
family and friends especially from Cherise. Weekends were
very difficult to get through because Calvin would drink
alcohol every weekend. His inner demons would surface and

act out whenever he drank. Calvin worked the four/ten scheduled which is four days a week and ten hours per day. He was off work Friday, Saturday, and Sundays. He expected me to walk in the door on Fridays with a meal from a restaurant for him; not at his expense, but mines. I explain to Calvin because I do all the house work cleaning and cooking and pay fifty percent of the bills, he should have dinner waiting for me when I get on Fridays. When we first got marry, he paid the rent and I paid the utilities and purchase the household items. Because of him complaining nonstop I agree to fifty percent of the bills and we each buy our own food. However, I was still purchasing the cleaning product because I was the only one cleaning the house. Over time, our weekend arguments became so intense, I stopped washing his clothes, cleaning his bathroom, and cooking for him. I made him feel the effect of the fifty-fifty rule.

Calvin never met my mother; however, he supports my decision to help her as much as I could. My mother had moved back to the Jordan Down projects. My brother Bow worked for Housing Authority but would never go visit our mother. Housing Authority would do yearly inspections on each apartment. After inspecting my mom's apartment, some of Bow co-workers told him that my mother's apartment was not up to living standards. Because of my work schedule and because Lenise was living in Los Angeles not far from where my mother lived, she would go check on mom for me. I must admit; I avoid visiting my mother because I wanted to force the hand of my brothers who lived near my mother. I was tired of being the responsible one. After the co-worker's complaint, Bow and his wife went one weekend to find that my mother's apartment was full of spider webs, mouse dropping and unclean kitchen and bathroom. They cleaned our mother's apartment and took over her banking to pay her behind bills. My mother had money in the bank but she was not paying her bills. We later found out my mother was blind due to cataracts from being a diabetic. No one knew how long she was blind because she would move around her apartment well without bumping into things. My mom would have Lenise fill out one of her checks for two hundred dollars and she would sign the check so that Lenise could cash the check to purchase food for my mother. Lenise did not know my mother could not see when she would check in twice a month to shop for her.

After Bow cleans our mom's apartment, he took over her finances and told Lenise that her services were no longer needed. Because Lenise was banned from going to check on my mom, I would call my mom weekly. Every third week of the month my mom would tell me that she did not have any food. She told me that my brother would buy her food on the first of the month only enough to last two weeks and he would not come back to check on her. She could not call my brother because she could see how to use her phone. Although we did not know she could not see, Bow should have checked in with mom to see if she needed anything since he was in control of her money. I would go to the neighborhood grocery store near where my mom lived to purchase food for her to last until Bow would shop for her on the first of the month. I never told my brothers that I was bringing food that I purchased with my money every third week of the month to our mother. To avoid arguing with them, I did what was needed in private. I did notice that I had to call my mother for her to open the door when I arrived. I did not think much of it because I assumed she was being caution as an elderly person living alone.

One day, mom fall on the kitchen floor. She was lying there for hours. My brother The Thief who normally does not go visit our mother had an urge to go see her. He kept banging on the door. He became nervous and decided to call Bow. Bow was the only family member who had a key to our mom's apartment. When Bow finally arrived at mom's place, they found her on the floor with a broken hip. Mom was rushed to the hospital. It was at the hospital my brothers were told that mom was blind due to cataracts. My mother was in a hospital three hours away from me scheduled to have hip replacement surgery. Mom repeatedly tells my brothers, Bow and The Thief, to call me; but they would not do it. Finally, a nurse asked Bow why was I not there, did I live out of town. Bow replied that he was our mom care taker and there was no need to contact me. The nurse explains that my presence could help her recovery because she wants to see me. Instead of Bow calling me, he calls Lenise and tell her about mom's surgery. Lenise called Cherise and me. My mom refused to go into surgery without me. By the time I arrived at the hospital, my daughters and brothers were waiting on me. My mom knew I was in the room as I approached her bed without anyone telling her I was there. She yelled my name with excitement. I could see my two brothers rowing their eyes and grunting. I ignore them and immediately embrace my mother with the tightness hug I could give her without hurting her. My mom told me that she loved me and she thank me for feeding her when she was hungry. I kissed my mom and told her I was happy God allowed me the means to be able to do it freely. My mom was at peace; her surgery was successful.

My mother was placed in a convalescent facility during her recovery. Because of the distance and traffic, I would go on weekends to visit. Lenise and Cherise would go on the weekdays. They would call me so that I could talk to my mom during their visit. My brothers never went to visit her while she was in the convalescent facility. They were too busy going through her personal item and trying to get her life insurance policy changed from my name as the beneficiary to Bow's name. Years ago, my mother had told me that I was the beneficiary on her life insurance policy. I had forgot about it and did not think about her dying after surgery.

Bow own two houses on the same street. He, his wife, Bow's young son, and the wife's young son lived in one of the houses. Bow's wife daughters lived in the other house with their kids. The house that Bow's stepdaughters lived in has a one-bedroom apartment in the back. Bow moved my mother into the one-bedroom apartment after she was released from the convalescent facility. I would go on weekends to visit my mother. Those visits were cut short; my mother died within a month of being released from the convalescent facility.

I received a call from Bow on a Sunday morning telling me that mom had died. He tells me that there was no need to come because mom's body was picked up about an hour ago by the mortuary and that arrangements were already made. What he said did not sit well in my spirit. I never knew of any funeral arrangements being made that soon immediately after the body was picked up. I had a knot in my gut that I could not find relieve. I decided to let go for the sake of peace. The next day on Monday, I received a call while I was at work on my cell phone. It was the mortuary director calling me asking me if he could do a conference call between the insurance company and myself. When I asked him the purpose of them needing to have a conference call with me; the director stated that I was the beneficiary on mother's insurance policy and that my brother Bow was in his office and needed permission to speak to the insurance rep. I gave the director permission for the conference call. Because the director had to call me back, it gave me time to take the call away from my desk in a private area of the building. After answering the director's call back, he announces that I was on a conference call with the insurance rep, himself and my brother who were sitting in the office. I had to say for the recorded call that I agree to all parties on the call. The insurance lady asked me some personal questions before asking me if my brother had permission to hear regarding the insurance policy. I said yes.

The insurance rep asked me for my permission to pay the mortuary that was handling my mother's burial. I gave my permission. I was then informed by the insurance rep that a balance of two thousand would be sent to me within three business day. I replied with okay, thank you. The mortuary director informed me that he would call me to come in and sign the paperwork once they receive the insurance payment. Again, I replied okay, thank you. The director stated they he was ending the conference call with me. I was getting ready to hang up when I heard my brother yelling in the back ground telling the insurance lady, "I told you I had permission from my sister to represent her." Although my brother lied about having my permission prior to the conference call, what I heard next made me weak in the knees. Bow tells the insurance lady, "you are trying not to pay me my money for my mother's heart attack. My mother died of a heart attack and the rider states if she dies of a heart attack I get five thousand dollars. You do not want to give me my money." The insurance rep tells my brother because the additional insurance is new, that he was not going to get a full five thousand. She explains after they get the coroner report they would make the adjustment, and that he would receive payment within five business days of the adjustment being made. At this point I hangs up the phone.

That evening, Bow calls me to say that he paid over two-thousand in cash to the mortuary and need me to reimburse him because he used his mortgage money to pay for our mother's burial. I told him that I will give him the two thousand once I receives the check and it clears the bank. I did not ask Bow about what I heard on the phone. I did not care; I just wanted this to be over with. Once the insurance check cleared my bank, I got a cashier check for two-thousand dollars and gave to my brother. After going to the mortuary and signing the paperwork for the insurance payment. The director gave me a list of items I need to bring for my mother to be bury in. On the paperwork I signed, it had me listed as the person paying but my brother list as the contact person over everything, including the burial at Inglewood Cemetery. There was something about the paperwork that did not add up. My mother went to

Inglewood Cemetery who handle the mortuary and burial for my younger sister and the cost was much greater. Anyhow after my mother service at the mortuary, we all had to drive our own cars to Inglewood Cemetery without police escort. Once we arrived, we stood in front of a casket in a hall way. A man spoke for ten minutes then it was over. Bow was telling his friends that the repast was being held at his house. He never told me and my kids. Myself, Calvin, and my kids all went to Sizzler near Inglewood Cemetery to eat before heading home.

I was so happy to make it through my mother's funeral without any arguments with my brothers. Little did I know at that moment of feeling relieved there was a storm to come. Two weeks after burying my mother, Bow calls me to ask me if he and his wife can come talk to me at my home. I said, "yes, you are welcome to come over anytime. My doors are always open to family." After hanging up the phone something hit me in the gut so hard I could physically feel it. I called Bow back and demanded to know why he needed to come to my home. Bow tells me that he just found another insurance policy for our mother and that I am the beneficiary. Then he proceeds to give me instructions on what he wants me to do, which is sign an affidavit for the insurance check to go to him or sign a document stating the insurance money is to be split among him, his wife, our brother The Thief and myself. I told him, "When hell freezes over; only then will I sign for thieves to get my mother's insurance money." Bow tells me that he will not give me the insurance policy until I sign the paperwork. I told Bow to kiss my whole ass after I have a good bowel movement; because I was not giving him and his goonies shit.

I spend the next few weeks calling different insurance companies trying to find my mother's insurance carrier. Those goonies put false information on my mother's death certificate as an attempt to keep me from getting a copy. They changed her birthday by one day and listed her brother as her father. Everything they meant for evil against me worked in my favor. After I decided to give up searching, The Thief called me to say that he did not have anything to do with Bow's actions, which I knew was a lie. I knew something was happening in the spirit realm for The Thief to suddenly come to me. I decided to try one more time to get a copy of my mother's dead certificate. With the false information listed on the certificate, I was able to get a copy giving them the correct information. The Thief tells me that he was able to convince Bow to give me the insurance policy and that he was bringing it over to me. I received a copy of the insurance policy and a letter attached to it from the insurance carrier stating that this is a fraud case that is in the process of being investigated. The letter was address to Bow at his address. I believe the insurance investigator told Bow sorry ass to give me the insurance policy or he would be arrested. The policy was for fifteen thousand dollars. I cried because they rob me of the opportunity to spiritually show my mother, I was going to properly take care of her in the same way she took care of my younger sister burial.

After the insurance check cleared my bank, Cherise and I went to Inglewood Cemetery to purchase a headstone for our mother's grave. I found out our mother was not buried at Inglewood Cemetery. I was told that she was at an unknown burial Crypt and that Inglewood Cemetery only handle the transport of the body. This is probably why I kept having dreams of my mother being in a cold dark stone dungeon in a foreign land. The staff at Inglewood showed me the paperwork that my brother Bow filled out. He listed only some of her children. I was not on the list. I was not allowed to have a memorial plate put on the wall at Inglewood Cemetery without my brother's permission. He was listed as the only owner of the crypt.

I decided to split ten-thousand dollars among my mother's grandkids in honor of her love for her grandkids. I took the remaining balance of five thousand and paid off my credit card debt. Each grandchild received a thousand-dollar cashier check in their name. Although I did give a cashier check to The Thief son, I did not give Bow three kids any money. I figure the four-thousand he stole from my three adopted kids covered his kids.

Twenty-two months after my mother death, my older sister dies. My sister had been sick for years. Her and I was employed in the same month and year with our first real job. In December of 1984 she was hired at McDonnell Douglas now known as Boeing. She worked as a Structural Mechanic. Although she used knee pads, years of crawling and working on her knees cause problems within her body. She had several carpal tunnel surgeries on her hands and wrist due to the continuous use of power tools. My sister was placed on a permanent medical leave with full pay and benefits from Boeing somewhere between the years 2010 to 2013. Her son was very close to his uncle's Bow and The Thief; therefore, he allowed them to talk him into handling his mother's funeral arrangements. For years my sister did not talk to Bow or The Thief and she would often tell her son that nothing good would come out of him having a relationship with them. As his surrogate mother until the age of five, I was a little hurt when I asked to assist my nephew with his mother arrangements and was turned down. Bow had not seen our sister since the age of sixteen. The Thief who had been in and out of jail all his life had not seen our sister since the year 2002. Our sister passed away in 2017. I was not surprised when The Thief had to call me to do the obituary because he did not know anything about our sister. I sent my nephew a copy of the obituary for his approval. Once my nephew approved, I let The Thief know all was good and approved for print. My nephew called me three days before the funeral to ask me if I was attending the repast at Bow's house. I told him no. He tried to talk me into it by saying, "do it for me auntie." I declined attending. Then my nephew said do it for my mom. I told him, "What I am doing is in honor of your mom. She did not like or trust Bow and The Thief, and she constantly warned you about them. They do not know her and I will not be socializing with them in her memory." Before hanging up, my nephew asked me to think about it. I said, okay for him.

Bow had chosen the same mortuary he used for our mother. There was no burial because my sister was cremated. The Thief asked one of his friends to preach a short message. The time of the funeral was off by thirty minutes; therefore, everyone had to wait until the room was ready. During the wait, Bow set up a large collage board for people to sign below the pictures. I asked someone, why are we signing this board; who are these people on the board. Someone said, these are pictures of the deceased lady. I say to this person, "I am the sister of the deceased lady, and not one of these pictures is of her. As a matter of fact, this picture right here with the lady wearing the Mitsubishi badge is a former co-worker of mines. Now I know who stole my tub of pictures." I was not trying to be funny, but the people within ear shot starts to laugh. Bow's wife was within ear shot and was trying to hide her laughter. I and my daughters low-key laughed. Those two clowns, Bow and The Thief, made a mockery of my sister's funeral. I believe many of the pictures on the Collage board was family on my mom's side. The ladies resemble my mother. Some of the ladies looked older than my mother which should have been a red flag in stating this is not our sister. And the clothes were from an era before my sister and I was born. I am not sure how my nephew felt about his mom's funeral. He could not sit still. He had a distraught look on his face. After the funeral, I hugged and kissed my nephew before leaving.

For years Calvin has been expressing that he wants us to move to the Inland Empire. I had declined each time he bought it up because I felt he was trying to isolate me from my family and friends. After my older sister funeral, Calvin expressed moving again. This time, I said yes. I needed a change. I told Calvin, I would move under one condition. The condition is that he would need to support the household one hundred percent until I find a job in the Inland Empire. I refuse to commute in traffic three to four hours one-way per weekday. On the weekends, Calvin and I went apartment searching in Fontana. We found a place on the border of Fontana and Rialto. We put in an application and was approved. After paying the security deposit, I put in a two week notice at my job Daylight Transport. My manager asked me why I was leaving the company. I told her that my husband and I was moving to the Inland Empire. She asked me which city in the Inland Empire. I told her Fontana. Daylight Transport had recently opened a warehouse in Fontana. The building had front office space for the departments that work directly with the drivers. A couple of days later my manager asked me to stay with the company and that they were working on finding me a desk and work area at the Fontana location. I agreed to withdraw my letter of resignation and work at the Fontana location. A month later, Calvin and I moved to Fontana.

Although our apartment in Fontana was a two-bedroom, two baths, it was much smaller than the apartment we moved from. Calvin work hours were 6:00am to 4:30pm. He got up at 2:00am and would leave home at 3:00am. He would arrive home between 7:00pm to 8:00pm. He would be so tire on his days off, Friday thru Sunday, he did not have energy to start his normal arguments over stupid stuff. All went well at home in the first year of living in Fontana. However, at work it was rocky for me. I was occupying a desk in the department that works with the drivers making sure all their paperwork was up-to-date, like license, certifications, and insurance. The manager of this department was looking to hire a new clerk. He asked Human Resources to offer me the position. I declined because it was paying six dollars less an hour. Me declining meant I was kicked out the department.

Besides empty offices for management, there were only two other departments in the building but a lot of empty space not used. The director over the drivers and warehouses did not want me to be in a space without supervision. The larger of the other two departments offer to allow me to use one of their desks. I was constantly watched every time I got up from my seat. I was time on how long I stayed in the bathroom. I was met with constant smart remarks from the director. The managers were okay with me until the director came around then they became a mini him. One day in front of all seating around me, the director picks up a very nasty dirty rubber band off the floor, he put the rubber band on my desk then he presses his thumb in my right shoulder blade with a great deal of force, as he says to me, "do not say I never gave you anything." As I looked around at everyone who witness what happen, they all dropped their heads in fear of this man. I knew at that moment I was not protected and it was time to leave the company. I found a job in two weeks; it was paying four dollar per hour less. I did not care. I accepted the job offer. Because I did not have anything personal in my desk or on my desk other than hand lotion. I did not go back to work once I accepted the job offer from the new company.

I decided to leave the Human Resource manager a voice mail as well as emailed my manager from my home computer stating that I had quitted due to being picked on and treated poorly. My phone was ringing non-stop from different people at Daylight Transport. I was in the process of getting my drug test done for my new job. I would listen to all the voice mails but I refused to call anyone back. Because this took place on a Friday, Calvin was off work. The CEO of Daylight Transport calls Calvin phone number to ask him to please have me call him directly. Because I always had great respect for the CEO, I decide to return his call. He has always been a fair person. He told me that he had knowledge of what the director did to me and that he would love for me to stay with the company working from home. This was music to my ears. Not only do I get to keep my pay rate, I get to keep my benefits and work from home. I was loving it. The CEO asked me if I would feel comfortable going back to the Fontana location for two weeks until they could arrange to have computers setup in my home. I told him that I did not feel safe going back to Fontana. This was on a Friday when I talk to the CEO. On Monday, I.T. was at my home before noon. It took I.T. less than thirty minutes to have me up and running. I was able to work half a day on that Monday.

My life is truly the essence of a Lifetime movie. Every time I climb up the mountain and take a deep breath, I am plunger right back down into the valley. I am still believing God for peace, joy, happiness, finance stability, protection from those who want to rob me of my peace and happiness in my golden years. Amen!

I am so at peace working from home; however, trouble shows its ugly face by targeting Calvin. Once a year for about six weeks, Calvin will work on Saturdays with the crew spraying the vegetation on the side of the freeways. Police escort is used when they work on the freeway. One Saturday, as Calvin was working. He was getting back in his truck to move up to spray the next area. As soon as he gets in his truck, in his side view mirror he could see this car coming straight for him. He made it in his truck seconds before the car hit the back of his truck. He did not have time to put his seat belt on before the impact. The police escort was approximately a fourth of mile behind Calvins work truck. The police were able to pin the woman car so that she could not take off. The woman was taken to jail for driving drunk. Calvin was taken to the hospital and was off work three weeks taking heavy pain medication. Although he had received the doctor approval to go back to work, the approval prohibits him from lifting heavy items which meant he was limited in preforming his job duties. Calvin's job accommodated him for a couple of months by having someone else do the heavy lifting. Because Calvin was still in pain the job felt Calvin should not be at work. They felt he should be on disability; they did not want him to get another worker's comp claim at the job. Therefore, every time he said he was in pain, they sent him home without pay. Calvin's job forces him through their actions to retire early, which meant he was not entire to his full pension. Also, Calvin's early retirement meant that I had to pick up financially what was once cover with his income. Because Calvin retired two years prior to qualifying for Medicare insurance, I had to add Calvin to my medical insurance with my job.

It was challenging working from home with Calvin being there every day. He did not respect the fact that I was at work between certain hours which means he should not call me to do things for him, or to come find things for him, or to answer none necessary questions; especially not walk in the spare bedroom where I work while I am in a virtual meeting for everyone to see him in the back ground. Every day I was arguing with Calvin because he was prohibiting me in doing my job well.

Because Calvin was in a great deal of pain and his injury was due to worker's comp, his primary doctor would not treat him or give him pain medication. Calvin went to see this Chinese lady who does acupuncture for pain relieve. She talked him into buying some herbs that look like cut up tree branches. He was required to boil these herbs for twenty-five minutes before drinking the tea from the herbs. I am very sensitive to the spirit realm. Those herbs were more than natural; they conjure up some dark spirits. Calvin eyes would turn blood red after drinking the tea. He would sit and stare at me with an evil look. I could not be in the house while Calvin boils his tea. I would sit on the patio until the smell dissipate from our apartment. I did not like the energy that came with the smell. I tolerated Calvin making tea for two weeks. Doing the course of those two weeks, we would hear weird sounds like someone walking in the hall dragging a ball and chain. Or, someone rolling a bowling ball in the hall. I begin to have nightmares every night of half human and half beast images. I had changed our bedding from flowers to our ruby red bed sheets. The next morning, the fitted sheet on Calvin's side of the bed was shredded like it was ripped with bear claws. One night I woke up standing in the hall near the guest bathroom without any knowledge of how I got there. Now that this darkness was starting to take control of my body it was time to take actions.

I threw away Calvin's tea and forbid him to purchase anymore. He cussed me out for throwing away his tea. He claims it was helping him and that he paid seventy-five dollars each week for the tea. I had to give him seventy-five dollars to stop the constant arguing about the money he loss from me throwing away his tea. He agreed to not purchase anymore tea. After throwing away the tea, I cleanse our apartment with white sage. I blessed our place with blessed olive oil. I would walk through our apartment every morning and evening praying and praising God and declaring in the powerful name of Jesus Christ that no dark spirits were welcome to occupy the same space as the spirit of God cover by his blood on the door post. After cleansing our apartment, I had a dream that in the city of Fontana was many dark spirits; these dark spirits, in the form of human like monsters, demons, and dark images were chasing me. I was running for my life. As I was running, I kept saying, "I got to get to Jesus." Me saying this repeatedly gave me the strength to keep running. Finally, I could see my apartment; the one where I was currently living. Jesus was standing at the threshold of the door. Within a few feet of me reaching the threshold, Jesus told me to stop. He tells me that my fear is what gives them power; then he says in a very powerful voice that was not loud, do not fear. Instantly fear left me.

Jesus told me to turn around; as I turned around, I could see thousands of dark spirits frozen in movement. They could not move because I had taken away their power by not fearing them. After the cleansing and the dream, our apartment was free of dark spirits.

Three months before our lease was to expired, we received a notice from the apartment complex offering us a one-year renewal at the same rate of rent or a two hundred dollar increase per month for a month-to-month lease. I told Calvin it was time to purchase our own home because rent was increasing yearly and we were getting too old to be moving every two years. Also, his fixed income was a little less than a thousand per month. I immediately contact the loan officer at my credit union for preapproval to purchase a house. I received the approval within a couple of days in applying for a mortgage loan. The loan officer referred me to a mortgage broker in the area where we were looking to live. The broker sent me four listings in the area. We agreed to meet the broker at the first listing on that coming Saturday morning. Calvin and I did not like the first two house. The third house felt like I belong there. I could see me living in the neighborhood and walking my future dog down the street. Calvin also liked the third house. We told the broker to make an offer for the asking price. Our offer was received. I wired the earnest money immediately after our offer was received. We closed escort in two weeks. My credit union did not want to put Calvin's name on the house because his income was low and was not needed to get the loan. Although Calvin and I had many problems and I was not in love with him, I could not do what they were suggesting to him. I told them to put his name on the house. We had two more months on our lease when we gave the apartment complex a thirty-day notice of us moving. The lady in the office gave us some grace on our lease. She said if we paid one more month in rent, she would excuse us from paying the last month of rent.

The move to our new home in Hemet was very rapid and draining. I was packing a house while I worked from home. I had to color tag all my work cords, monitors, controller so that I would know how to put it back together in-order to not have someone from I.T travel three hours to Hemet. I did not trust the mover moving my work system. I carefully packed the work system, the night before the move, and place the system in my car the morning of the move. Taking only the Friday of the move and the Monday after the move off work, allowed me the time I needed to setup my office at the new location after the cable company had set up the WIFI the next day after the move. It took me almost a month to unpack all the boxes.

Six months after living in our home, Calvin had an outpatient procedure schedule. The procedure was cosmetic in nature. Calvin refuses to find a primary doctor closer to where we lived. His doctor was over an hour away without traffic. He scheduled this procedure without checking with my work schedule or letting me know in advance. Because the procedure requires anesthesia he needs a driver. I told Calvin that I cannot take off work. He proceeds to argue that all I do is sit on my ass all day and type on the computer. Therefore, he cannot understand the need to give notice. I tell Calvin, me sitting on my ass all day typing is paying the bills. Calvin tells me that I need to pay the bills because we would not have the house if he did not co-sign for me to get the house. I told him that I was not going to argue with a delusional person. It was senseless. I asked my daughter Cherise if she could come and take him to his appointment. Because Cherise did not have a car at the time she had to take the Amtrack train from downtown Los Angeles to Riverside. I pick her up at the station after getting off work.

The next day after picking up Cherise, Calvin received a call from the doctor's office stating that the insurance had declined approval for his cosmetic surgery. Because Cherise had pre-purchased her return ticket she had to stay until that Saturday, which was two day later. Calvin got drunk the next day after getting his call from the doctor. That evening of him getting drunk, I was babysitting my oldest son three kids. The kids were sitting on the floor watching TV. Cherise was sitting at the dining room table talking to me as I prepared dinner. Suddenly Calvin gets up after drinking two bottles of wine and some dark brown liquor, gets in Cherise face and cuss her out. He tells her, "You think you are your mama; that is your probably, you want to be your mama, and you think you are her." At this point, Cherise gets ready loud like she was trying to drown his voice. She was screaming at him saying, "F-you nigga, what are you going to do nigga." I turn off the stove and stood between them. I told Calvin to go sleep off the alcohol. He threatens to kill everyone in the house if Cherise did not shut the F-up. I told Calvin that I was going to call the police if he did not go sleep off the alcohol. He goes in the room shouting I know you got a knife behind your back. I am going into the room because I know you got a knife behind your back. I did not have a knife behind my back. I did not correct what he was saying because him believing I had a knife is what cause him to go sleep it off. Cherise never spent the night at my home after the blow up between her and Calvin. Whenever her and I would hang out in my area, Cherise would get a hotel room.

Life was livening as normal. Calvin and I are arguing more than normal due to him drinking to numb the pain in his back. My youngest daughter Lenise and her long-term boyfriend, the father of her kids, where moving to California City in a house her boyfriend purchased. Things were going as planned until the last day of them moving. A child protective service social worker shows up at the apartment they were moving from. The worker asked to see the kids. The kids were not available. The worker asked to come into the apartment. Lenise told the worker we moved; we are here to pick up the few items that is left; therefore, Lenise declined to allow the worker to come into the apartment. The worker looks through the window then writes on her pad as she speaks out loud, "your place is not safe for kids, it is unsanitary with trash everywhere." Lenise repeated what she previously said to the worker, "we do not live here anymore, we moved. We are only here to pick up a few items that was left behind." The worker demanded to see the kids. Lenise repeated, "they are not here." The worker asked for their new address. Because the address was in California City, Kerns County, the worker said that the kids cannot be taken from Los Angeles County. Lenise tells the worker if you need to see my kids come to California City because my kids are going with me. The worker tells them to not leave as she calls the police. Lenise and the father of the kids left. As they were driving to their new house, Lenise cell phone rings. It was the police telling her if she does not bring her kids to the court hearing on that coming Friday, she will be arrested for kidnap.

Lenise calls me hysteric about what happen. I am trying to wrap my brains around what she is saying. I am thinking how did it get to this point where you all have a court date and this is your first encounter with a social worker. I am baffle; but, at the same time I do not want to add any more stress to her life with all the questions going on in my mind. Lenise asked me, "mom what should I do." I tell her you must go to court with the kids as they instructed you. The court hearing was held in downtown Los Angeles. I live in Riverside County and work from home. It would have taken me over four hours to attend court with Lenise and the father of the kids. I had to sit this one out and wait for Lenise call to give clarity on what is going on. Lenise called me crying saying that they took her kids from them at court. The kids were placed with Ms. A's son who was listed on the paperwork as their only relative. I was livid. The actions of the court tell me that a buildup of occurrences and socializing with Ms. A had to take place, that I have no knowledge about, for it to get to this point.

The grandkids being taken by an outsider bought the family together. My brother Bow heard about it and got involved in a positive way. I learned from my three adopted kids that Ms. A had been talking negatively about me to them for years. She would tell them that I only adopted them for the money; like $345 dollars per month for each was going to make me rich. Although by the time the kids reach age eighteen, I was receiving $585 dollar per month for each. The agency gave a small increased every five years per adopted kid. I found out because I was a relative of the kids and not a license foster parent is the reason I received less money per month than license foster parents. I was okay with it because it was never about the money. Also Ms. A told the kids that I did not love them like I love my own birth son. After the kids got older and looked back on the life I provided for them, they realized that Ms. A was lying about my intentions in adopting them. I was hurt that the kids had this knowledge and did not tell me, and continued to socialize with someone who is clearly lying on me.

With all that I have been through in life, this was the first time I built hate in my heart towards someone. It is one thing to attack me, I can handle her personal attacks on me; but when she came for my family; my grandbabies, I went somewhere in my mind that scared me. Because I refused to allow that devil my adversary to separate me from the God that I love, I had to pray day and night asking God to help me. I had to hold on to the love in my heart for God to function daily in the light of God and not act on the thoughts that was in my mind. I would cry daily in private because I did not want anyone to know how much I was hurting. I would read my bible daily; listen to praise and gospel music daily; and of course, pray daily. It took a long time before the hate being to dissipate. I knew my heart was changing when I begin to feel sorry for Ms. A. It was at this moment I understood the scripture in Matthew 5:44, "But I say to you, love your enemies, bless those who curse you, do good to those who hate you and pray for those who spitefully use you and persecute you." What Ms. A do not understand is that no one is exempt from reaping what they sow in life. We always reap greater than what we sow; therefore, if someone is sowing good, they would reap more or receive more than what they sowed. If they sow evil; they would receive a greater return in the evil they sowed.

My family learned that Ms. A lied to a church member who works in a high position in Child Protection Service (CPS) to gain knowledge on what to do to get custody of my daughter's kids. There was a two-year book of document pages given to Lenise at court showing the time, and date of people; the same three people numbers, calling CPS with complaints about the safety of Lenise's kids. The callers stated that they were the only relatives of the kids. Also, the two-hundred-page paperwork stated that Ms. A son was the only uncle. Because myself and my oldest son, who was willing to take the kids, lived in a different county, CPS allowed my brother Bow background check clearance be used in getting the kids back with the family. The kids lived with Bow for two years before the case was closed. My grandson is still dealing with the aftermath of being taken from his parents.

Dealing with the CPS situation took my mind away from Calvin foolishness. I just did not have the energy to argue with him or give his complaining about nonsense any attention. Because of allergies, my nose would itch and I would sneeze a lot. I formed a habit in pushing up my nose with my hand whenever my nose would itch. It caused me to get a brown crease line across my nose. I used whitening cream to remove the brown line by blending the complexion on my nose. The use of whitening cream causes me to have sinus problems such as snoring. Although Calvin is a chronic snorer, and has been since the day we met, he begins to complain about me snoring. One day I woke up in a panic because Calvin was pressing a pillow to my face cutting off my air. From that day forward I slept in the guest bedroom where I worked.

After I retired from Daylight Transport Calvin became very strange in his behavior. I believe the change in his behavior was due to him seeing me at the same financial level as him. Although my income was still greater than his, me being on a lower income put me in the same position as him financially. This gave Calvin a security in believing that I could not or would not leave him because we both could not afford to live without the other person's income. And because we both were tied to the commitment of owning a house. Calvin begins to talk to me crazier than normal, disrespect me by cussing me out of front of people publicly. Although we had automatic sprinter to water the grass, he would intentionally go outside to water the grass so that he can step in mud from the flower bed then track the mud throughout the house without cleaning it up. He would intentionally spill liquid and food on the kitchen floor, drop crumbs around the dining room table when he ate and on the living room floor while eating snacks. He would leave clothes all over the house and never throw away his junk mail. It would be piles of junk mail all over the house.

Calvin begins to make a few dollars by driving this guy around town to run errands. This person lived about five miles away in a huge house with other people in the same religion as him. Their religion did not believe in eating meat. They would talk and teach Calvin about their religion. Calvin would come home with pamphlets and small books about what they believe. Calvin would talk to them about our relationship. They kept telling Calvin to invite me to come visit with them so that they could counsel us as a couple. I refused. Calvin did not know the name of their religion; yet he was studying with them. I believe Calvin went to some type welcoming ceremony with this religious group. For three consecutive Saturdays, Calvin claimed he needed to help this guy do some work at midnight in the mountains. Calvin would take a change of clothing each time he went.

The clothing would be a button-down dress shirt and dress slacks. After completing the three consecutive Saturdays, Calvin begins to put something in my food. One time I made tuna salad, enough for two days. The second day I tasted it; the taste was extremely different. I could not eat it. Because Calvin cooked separately, I would always prepare enough food for the next day so that I would only need to cook every other day. Every time I would eat my food on the second day, I would get sick. When I stop preparing enough food for a second day; Calvin begins to tamper with my seasoning, causing me to get sick every time I ate. I decided it was time to put a ring camera in the kitchen. This was the only way to keep Calvin from tampering with my food.

One day I went shopping, Calvin was in my room on my computer when he heard me come into the house. He jumps up so fast from my computer to ran out my room that he broke my laptop computer to the point where the top would not fold into a close position. The ring camera recorded several videos of Calvin talking to himself in an argumentative way. It was like he was having a verbal argument with someone in his mind because no words were recorded. On one of these occasions, a dark spirit came out Calvin's body and linger around him for a few seconds before returning into his body. I saved this video to my google account and showed the video to my kids so that they would be a witness that it was not my imagination. I still have that video. I no longer felt safe in my home. I immediately file for divorce and had Calvin served with divorce papers. After he was served, I put the house on the market for sale; because I did not trust Calvin to keep the house presentable for people coming in and out to view the house, I decided to have Open Door gives us a quote in purchasing our house. Open Door quoted us ninety thousand over what we owed on the house. I accepted the offer. I choose a thirty day close which gave us enough time to pack.

After signing the final paperwork with Open Door showing that fifty percent of the proceeds would get deposited into our separate bank accounts, Calvin rented a U-Haul truck and took all the furniture with him to Arizona to live with his daughter. I had movers move my things into storage. Cherise and I had been talking about wanting to move out of California. I had applied for several senior apartments in California. All had two to three years waiting list. Cherise decided to apply for a VA loan. She was approved but did not have any money to pay the down payment or closing cost. I was living in an Air B and B. when

Cherise asked me to move in with her. I was hesitant but at this point I had no other choice. I was homeless but free from Calvin. Cherise tried to find a condo or townhouse in California for the amount she was approved. California had nothing below three hundred thousand. We were force to look outside the state. We both agree on Texas. We look at several cities in Texas. I total Cherise let go to Houston because I hear the food in Houston is good, plus it a huge diverse city that welcome all as equal. We both said, "Houston here we come." Cherise was able to find a new built three-bedroom, two full baths with an office for less than what she was approved for from the VA. My half of the proceeds were used to purchase Cherise's house, move us from California to Texas, and purchase all the furniture in Cherise house. Within two years after moving to Texas I was broke and living in my daughter's house on a fixed social security income.

I knew living with Cherise would be challenging based on her short attention span. One minute she is like an adult child wanting to play and prank people with her sense of humor that is not funny to others. The next minute she wants to invade your peace of mind talking about world interest that does not interest the listener. If a person does not cater to her interest, she becomes agitated with them, which at times leads to her putting the person out her house. Cherise is not good on receiving the truth about her split personality. She gets highly upset and become argumentative. Therefore, I cannot say that I did not know what I was getting into when I agree to live with Cherise. Whenever Cherise would feel lonely, she would invite Lenise and her kids to come hang out with her for a couple of days. Lenise would never make it more than a day before she is calling me complaining about Cherise up and down mood swings. I always tried to encourage Lenise to be the bigger person by hanging in there. After moving to Texas with Cherise I had to eat the words I spoke to Lenise by being the bigger person.

What I discover by living with Cherise is not only does she have major up and down mood swings; as an Army Veteran she is dealing with Post-Traumatic Stress Disorder (PTSD). For the first year living in Texas with Cherise, I went along with her controlling rules and mood swings. She did not want me to drive myself anywhere. She had to drive me. I believe the reason I went along with her control on driving me everywhere is because Texas roads confused me. I decided to challenge myself by learning how to navigate through the Houston streets by using GPS. Cherise would always ask me where I was going and the location of where I was going. My go to stores were Walmart or Costco. After telling Cherise where I was going, I would see her there watching me from a far. On one occasion I told Cherise that I was going to Walmart but I end up going elsewhere. When I returned home, Cherise reprimand me because she came to Walmart and did not see me and did not see my car in the parking lot. I told Cherise that she was acting like a stalker and it needed to stop. Well, I guess my request for her to stop stalking me caused her to become aggressive in a nonphysical way.

Cherise would show her aggression towards me by throwing away my food. I would purchase a full half of Salmon from Costco and cut it into five to six serving sizes. Cherise would throw my salmon away in the outside trash can. This is only one example of the many different food of mines that she threw away. On one occasion I was looking for my mangos. I figure she had thrown them away. About a week after looking for my mangos, I was driving to Walmart when this nauseating smell was in my car. It smells like a dead animal. The smell caused me to turn around and head back home. It was too hot outside to roll down the windows;

the air condition did not help the smell. When I arrived home, I put on some rubber gloves and grab the Clorox wipes to see if I spilled something on the floor of the car. The smell led me to look under the passenger seat. Guess what I found; my mangos. Cherise had put my mangos in my hot car to rot. I know for a fact that I did not forget to take my mangos out the car; because, after putting away my groceries, I had a conversation with Cherise about the mangos. I did not want Cherise to think they were her mangos because I do not normally eat mangos; but I was making a special dish that I saw on TV, and I had shown Cherise where I was putting my mangos.

Cherise's nonphysical aggression moved to my bedroom. Because Cherise did not like sleeping in the back of the house, she gave me the master bedroom with a full bath. While I was running errands, Cherise would go in my room and take things of value to me. After several things came up missing, I changed my regular door knob to a door knob lock with a key to unlock from the outside. Cherise would pick the lock. It was obvious to me that she was picking the lock, became each time she did, it was difficult for me to put the key straight into the lock. I had to purchase a dead bolt lock to keep her from picking the lock. Talking to

Cherise about what she was doing always result in her gaslighting me by trying to convince me that it was in my mind. She would say my senior mind was playing tricks on me. I got to the point where I just did not care anymore about my food. I would pray daily for God to allow me to find an apartment that was accommodating to my fixed income. I applied for a HUD senior apartment. I was not sure if I would qualify because when I check the income limit to qualify, it showed that I received forty dollars a year over the limit. I decided to apply anyway. I am happy that I did apply for the HUD senior apartment, because the income limit, I was looking at was for a previous year. Let me tell you, after I moved into my senior apartment, I praised God like he had given me a new house of my own mortgage free. I was and still is very grateful for my apartment and for my peace.

After moving to Texas several men would approach me. I was not interested in dating. This one guy who is four years older than myself lived an hour away from my home in Sugarland approached me in the downtown area of Houston. I decided it would be safe in giving him my phone number just for adult conversation; because, we both had expressed that we do not like driving too far away from home. We talked on the phone every day. We met twice at a restaurant between where we lived. I realized that I was nitpicking and looking for similarities to my past relationships. He made a statement to me that sound like something the ex-husband would say. I immediately told him not to call me anymore. It was at this moment I knew it was time to heal from my past relationships. I begin to spend time daily with God in meditation, as well as, praying, reading my bible, listening to praise music as I praise God for the victory.

In my journey to heal I begin to look back on what caused me pain in my relationships. I realized it all originate from the rape at age eighteen. That rape had cripple me by causing me to draw to myself men who was identical to my rapist. It was difficult but I knew I had to see myself as someone who is deserving of having someone in my life who authentically loves me and who I can feel love for him. I had to forgive myself for believing that it was my fault. I had to assure myself that I was not too old to have love in my life and enjoy all the amenities that comes with love. I told God that I want to know what love feels like and I want it to be with someone who will not hurt my heart. I told God that I will trust him and the process in attracting love into my life. I got up every day and praise God for love coming into my life and for bringing a good man into my life.

Well, six months after moving to Texas, I was preparing to fly back to California for a cruise that I had preplanned over a year in advance when I got this gut feeling to contact Leonard; my first boyfriend at age seventeen. Lenoard and I had been friends on Facebook since 2011. I knew he was married so I had to choose my words respectfully. I wanted to see if he could help me recall lost memory. I thought by recalling or regaining the lost memory would give me the power to overcome the pain of it so that my heart will no longer react to the pain of what I cannot remember. I sent Leonard a message on Facebook Messenger with my phone number. I explain to Leonard that I would be returning home on May 7th 2024. Leonard called me on May 10th. I talked to him briefly about my healing journey and how I hope he could bring some clarity about the past. Leonard helped me with some understanding; however, like me he could not recall much. Before hanging up the phone, I told Leonard about being taken advantage of by our former manager. Leonard was the one who called it what it was; rape. I was scare to use the word rape with Leonard. I was happy when he used it first. It let me know that he heard me and still was that compassionate caring person I always known him to be. We talked a little about me moving to Texas. He told me that his wife had died and a little about what he was doing. As we were getting ready to end our call, Leonard asks if he could take me to lunch or dinner the next time he comes to Texas. Within out hesitating I said yes. What Leonard did not know is that I was feeling butterflies in my stomach as we talked. I had not felt anything like that since Leonard and I dated at the age of seventeen. The next month after talking to Leonard, I flew to California to spend the weekend with Leonard. He would have flown to Texas if he did not have to work late on that Friday or go into work early on that coming Monday. Nevertheless, he made up for it. Leonard started flying to Texas every other month; sometimes he would come back-to-back. To this date, Leonard and I are committed to each other. We are discussing taking our relationship to the next level. I now know what love feels like. To God Be the Glory!

About the Author

Judy Owens is a mother, and a grandmother, who is currently living in Texas. She is an avid reader who has always desired to share her wisdom in print. Judy's love for reading began at the age of fifteen after reading her first book, The Diary of Anne Frank. Throughout the years, reading has taken Judy into a place of serenity, where she visions the world through someone's creative thoughts on print. Judy's hope is to enrich the life of the reader.